MAST BROTHERS CHOCOLATE

A FAMILY COOKBOOK

1.

Cacao Tree
ready for
harvest

2.

Cacao pods

seeds
"beans"

5.

Beans are Sailed to Brooklyn
from around the world.

USA

NYC

DR

6.

Roast
beans
delicately!

MAST BROTHERS CHOCOLATE
Brooklyn, NY

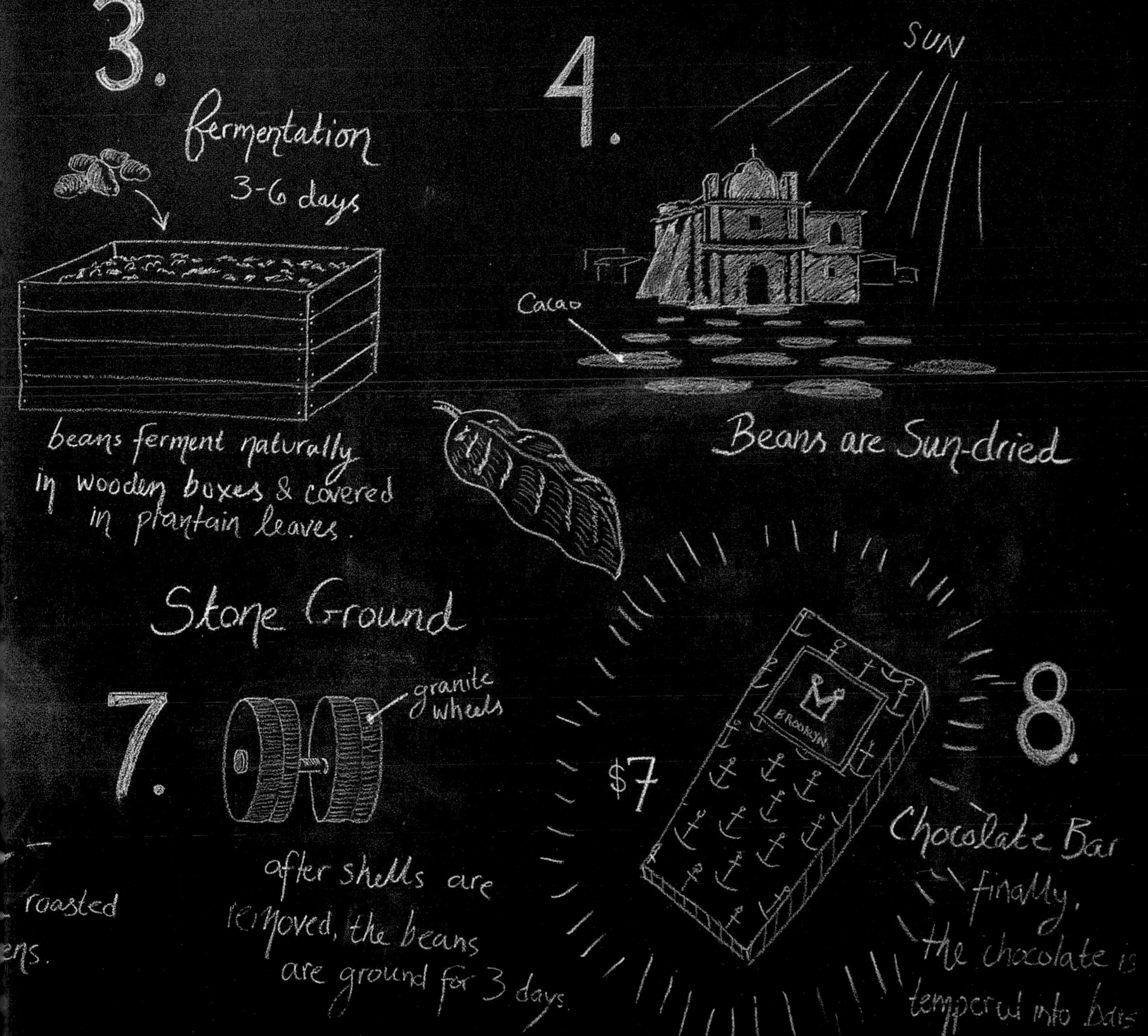

3.

Fermentation
3-6 days

beans ferment naturally
in wooden boxes & covered
in plantain leaves.

4.

SUN

Cacao

Beans are Sun-dried

Stone Ground

7.

granite
wheels

after shells are
removed, the beans
are ground for 3 days.

roasted
ens.

$7

8.

Chocolate Bar
finally,
the chocolate is
tempered into bars

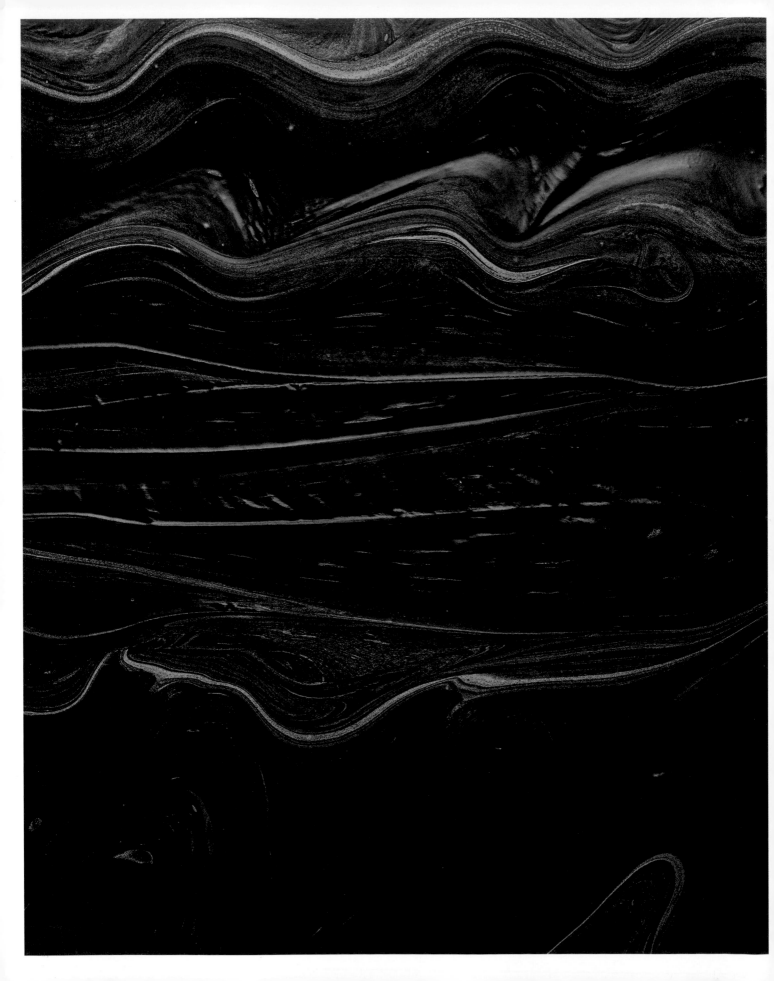

MAST BROTHERS CHOCOLATE
A FAMILY COOKBOOK

RICK MAST & MICHAEL MAST

Foreword
by Thomas Keller

Photography
by Tuukka Koski

Little, Brown and Company
New York Boston London

Little, Brown and Company
Hachette Book Group
237 Park Avenue, New York, NY 10017
littlebrown.com
First Edition: October 2013

Little, Brown and Company is a division of Hachette Book Group, Inc.
The Little, Brown name and logo are trademarks of Hachette Book Group, Inc.

The publisher is not responsible for websites (or their content) that are not
owned by the publisher.

The Hachette Speakers Bureau provides a wide range of authors for speaking events.
To find out more, go to hachettespeakersbureau.com or call (866) 376-6591.

ISBN 978-0-316-23484-9
LCCN 2013938865
10 9 8 7 6 5 4 3 2 1

SC

Art direction: Nathan Warkentin
Design: Jennifer S. Muller
Printed in China

To our mother, we love you

CONTENTS

FOREWORD *1*
Thomas Keller

INTRODUCTION *5*
The Seven Crowns | Craft Chocolate | Tempering Chocolate

PART ONE: THE BEGINNING *11*
Food Memories | Finding Chocolate

PART TWO: SOURCING & GATHERING *43*
A Cacao Farmer | The Maine Coast

PART THREE: SAILING FOR CACAO *73*
Finding a Boat | Out to Sea | The Brooklyn Waterfront

PART FOUR: MASTERING OUR CRAFT *119*
A Factory Grows in Brooklyn | Making Craft Chocolate | Wrap Your Chocolate Like Food

PART FIVE: MARKETS & GROCERS *159*
Going Public | It Takes a Village | Butchers

PART SIX: THE CHEFS *203*
A Surprise Visitor | First Best Meal

PART SEVEN: COMMUNITY *229*
An American Collaboration | Lunch Break | Hootenannies

THANK YOU *265*

METRIC CONVERSIONS *268*

INDEX *271*

FOREWORD

by Thomas Keller

In 2007 our French Laundry pastry chefs returned from a trip to New York, excited to tell the story of two chocolate makers they'd met. Rick and Michael Mast were born and raised in Iowa but now lived in Brooklyn, where they carried out their craft like urban alchemists, roasting cocoa beans in their Williamsburg apartment, cracking them by hand, using a hair dryer to separate the nibs from the shells. They hand wrapped their confections in artful paper and sold them on weekends at farmers' markets around the region—a near full-time commitment that they stuck to without giving up their day jobs. Rick earned his keep working in the kitchens of New York's top restaurants. Michael worked in film production.

Their story was a good one. But the skeptic in me wondered if theirs was just another tale of hipster hobbyists riding the artisanal small-batch bandwagon.

Then I met them at their factory in New York, and my doubts faded away.

I could tell that they were men who shared my sensibilities, who worked with a rigor that bordered on obsession because that was the only way they knew. They sourced their ingredients meticulously and refined their recipes over and over until they arrived at the right results. Just as I'd planted my own restaurant garden at The French Laundry to ensure the quality of my signature ingredients, Rick and Michael had cultivated close relationships with small farmers around the world whose commitment came through in everything they produced. The Mast Brothers were loyal to their farmers, and that loyalty was returned in kind. I was happy to learn that the owner of the Madagascar farm from which they source cocoa beans often attends their company holiday party; they make annual trips to Belize and the Dominican Republic. Cooperatives in those countries, which the Masts visit annually, have

now become business models for other farmers to emulate.

Like many who meet Rick and Michael for the first time, I was struck by their height. Both are six three. But what really stands out is their stature. They are pioneers in the bean-to-bar movement. The Masts have earned wide-ranging accolades for their chocolate, which is only fitting. Their work is artisanal. It's also ethical. They go beyond Fair Trade to direct trade and have personal relationships with each farmer—eliminating any third party by sourcing directly.

All of these qualities are evident in this book. It's their first, and like everything they do, it's been produced with care. In it, Rick and Michael don't just share their recipes. They share stories about each item's significance—delicious accompaniments to each dish.

As it is for many, chocolate is a childhood favorite of mine. I believe in its Proustian powers, having sensed them in the whiff of piping hot cocoa crowned with whipped cream, and in the bite of a decadent birthday cake blanketed in swirls of fudgy frosting. Here, Rick and Michael introduce a selection of refined specialties—like mole, chocolate barbecue sauce, and cocoa coq au vin—that stir special memories for them. But the recipes here—check out their take on a chocolate egg cream—are also apt to conjure your own special recollections and help you create new memories in your own home.

Living by guiding principles they call the Seven Crowns—pillars for their company and their lives—has helped them make sound decisions and achieve great success. The first crown is to honor the importance of family.

There is authenticity and accountability behind the brand, not a faceless pool of venture capitalists and investors. Curiosity and discovery drive them each day, and the brothers continually challenge themselves and their staff to learn more about chocolate and to develop new skills.

We are forever enriched by people like the Mast Brothers, who have helped us appreciate the range of flavors possible in a single bar of chocolate. In return, I believe, we owe them our support. The payoff, after all, works both ways. As you turn these pages, I encourage you to take Rick's advice:

"Shake it up and evolve. Be fearless and experiment. Embrace continuous improvement in the pursuit of ultimate simplicity."

THE SEVEN CROWNS

Early on, we knew that we were onto something. Something that had the potential to inspire and change the way a lot of people thought about chocolate, about food, about community engagement, and about building a business. We determined that great businesses are built on more than just outstanding products; they are built on an outstanding sense of culture and principles. So we set out to articulate our ideas, facilitating and guiding our growth, a principled growth.

The seven crowns serve us well, providing criteria for decisions both large and small. It is outrageously easy to justify any decision without a set of guidelines, so our crowns provide a decision-making framework for our entire company.

Love, respect, and serve family and community.
Give, inspire, and serve those around you—your coworkers and customers,
your drinking buddies, and your actual family. Everyone deserves the
best of what you can give!

Master your craft.
Continuously improve the quality of your craft. Work cleaner and smarter.
Taste more and explore more. Ask questions. Demand excellence of
yourself when no one is looking.

Make everything delicious.
The chocolate, the packaging design, the lighting, the culture, the meticulous
cleanliness of the factory—everything must be delicious.

Waste nothing.
We strive to be a zero-waste manufacturer. We also mustn't waste time or energy,
so we are committed to working with efficiency and intelligence.

Connect customers to the source.
We are nothing without our farmers. In every way possible, we must pay tribute to
them and share their work. Connect the dots.

Innovate through simplicity.
Breathe. The urge to complicate is an urge to avoid the obvious. Stop finagling and
bring clarity to your work and peace to your spirit.

Be honest and transparent.
We demand integrity in everything we do and eagerly open ourselves up to the
world with pride. That's why we opened a craft chocolate factory in the
middle of New York City!

There they are. We know they seem simple, maybe even obvious. That is why we love them so much. They are our road map, and we would be lost without them. —*RM & MM*

CRAFT CHOCOLATE

We live in a time when consumers want to know the origins of their heirloom tomatoes, the diet of the cows butchered for their burgers, and the first name of their local brewer. Chocolate somehow has avoided this microscope. The large majority of all chocolate is uniformly bland, loaded with poor ingredients, and made by only a few companies, on a mega-industrial scale. Iconic American brands make their chocolate overseas, focusing entirely on saving money and increasing yields rather than on sourcing better ingredients, nurturing relationships with farmers and producers, and making a higher-quality, more delicious chocolate.

At Mast Brothers, we handcraft chocolate in a way that seeks to highlight the unique characteristics of its exceptional ingredients, cacao and sugar. Ingredient-focused cooking always respects the process in its entirety: from ground to mouth, farmer to customer, bean to bar. We have never created and will never create a product that simply facilitates existing industrial manufacturing techniques but instead seek to handcraft chocolate in a way that results in the most delicious chocolate.

Despite consisting of simply two ingredients, beans and sugar, chocolate has an inspiringly wide range of flavor notes. As is the case with wine, these flavor notes depend largely on tree (and therefore bean) varietal, soil conditions, biodiversity, farming techniques, and weather conditions. It is these variables that make a Madagascar single-estate chocolate so over-the-top citrusy while Venezuelan-origin chocolate tends to be mellower, with notes of molasses, cinnamon, and dark berries.

Because of the simplicity of its ingredients, craft chocolate has a lower fat content than conventional chocolate and does not contain any emulsifiers. What this means is that craft chocolate is far more complex in flavor but can be more difficult to temper. When cooking with it, adjustments must be made to account for the additional cocoa butter content found in conventional chocolate. The recipes in this cookbook do just that. That said, the recipes will work equally well for Mast Brothers chocolate as for the high-quality dark chocolate of your choice. Experiment and see for yourself; let your taste buds be your guide.

When the recipes call for dark chocolate, look for a chocolate that contains over 70 percent cocoa solids. This will provide the intensity of flavor and appropriate cocoa butter content to properly execute the recipe. It is rare to find a fine chocolate under the 70 percent range that doesn't have added butters.

When choosing a dark chocolate to cook with, pick one that you would eat on its own. Choose a chocolate from people you know and trust. Most important, taste and experiment. Eat what you like, but challenge and educate your palate. After all, we never knew we liked chocolate until we had *good* chocolate. Now we have dedicated our lives to the pursuit of making the best chocolate we can.

TEMPERING CHOCOLATE

Tempering chocolate is an essential skill for many of the recipes included in this book. It is a process that stabilizes the cocoa butter, giving melted chocolate its beautiful glossy sheen and crisp snap; an unstable, untempered chocolate will turn streaky and gray. Tempering also raises the chocolate's melting point, which is very handy for prolonged storage.

Tempering chocolate can be a highly scientific and complex process and an entire book could easily be written about tempering, but for the purposes of executing these recipes in a home kitchen, we describe here a very simplified method.

Step 1: Melt the chocolate.
Using a double boiler, melt dark chocolate to between 115 and 118 degrees Fahrenheit. Stir constantly, ensuring that the entire batch is melted to the appropriate temperature.

Step 2: Cool the chocolate.
Remove the bowl of melted chocolate from the heat. Slowly add and incorporate chopped pieces of chocolate, stirring constantly until the temperature of the chocolate reaches 83 degrees Fahrenheit. If pieces of solid chocolate remain, you can use a handheld blender to smooth everything out.

Step 3: Reheat the chocolate.
Put the bowl of chocolate back onto the double boiler, and bring the temperature of the chocolate to between 88 and 90 degrees Fahrenheit, stirring constantly. Use immediately, as the chocolate will only remain in temper for as long as it stays within this temperature range.

– Part One –

THE BEGINNING

FOOD MEMORIES

"There is no sincerer love than the love of food."
—George Bernard Shaw

———————

Long before the question "How is chocolate made?" crossed our lips—and when the people and farms of Central America were no more real to us than bedtime stories—our attention was focused on Iowa, our birthplace, the place that set the stage for my love affair with food.

Our father had suffered from bouts of manic depression and alcoholism, and it drove our parents apart when I was four and my brother, Michael, was two. Leaving our father behind, along with the house he had built by hand and the small farm town of Primghar, was difficult, but our mother maintained our connection to our birthplace with many trips, often in the summer months, to spend time with our father's parents. This kept us connected both to the earth and to our past, although our mother would never phrase it like that—we were just going to Grandma and Grandpa's house, because that's what people did.

Our mother's 1979 blue Mercury Cougar grumbled west on I-80 from our new life and home in Iowa City. She drove with a stiff left arm and clenched jaw, her white knuckles topping the wheel. Her right arm was equally tense but provided a protective hand on my side as I lay with my head on her lap, counting the rhythmic beat of the wheels going over breaks in the pavement against the beat of Phil Collins's "Against All Odds" and Springsteen's "Glory Days." Michael and our older sister, Anne Marie, were in the back and had built nests of pillows and quilts on the floor, leaving room on the seat to stage intergalactic wars, race cars, and draw in coloring books.

We were greeted by a sign that proudly stated "Primghar: The Only One in the World." It was a six-hour drive to Grandma Clara and Grandpa Elmer's Victorian farmhouse in Primghar. Two stories with a wraparound porch, covered in sage vinyl siding faded by sun and the dusty wind that swept in from the gravel road. The house was filled with antiques: cast-iron kitchenware, grandfather clocks, an old bubble gum machine, Edwardian tables, and Shaker chairs with hutches of all shapes and sizes. Some were brought to Iowa by our ancestors in a covered wagon; others were picked up at the local auction house. Our grandpa, like our father, was a carpenter and furniture restorer, so their collection overflowed into the large detached garage. Boxes and tangled tables and chair legs covered a '64 Ford Thunderbird that had but 7,000 miles on it, used only to go to the grocery store and back, with the occasional trip to the family dentist.

On and around my grandparents' property were thriving victory gardens. It was from these immaculately kept miniature farms that I discovered for myself peaches that exploded with dripping flavor, the crisp tang of freshly picked radishes, and the joy of husking sweet corn on a hot August day. These gardens were utopias preserved from the surrounding corn lots, fantasy islands in the sea of industrial agriculture.

The soil was rich and the plantings were diverse. Sweet corn, yes, but there were also strawberries, cucumbers, raspberries, radishes, rhubarb, asparagus, sprouts, and rows of various lettuces and kale. The damp air carried the aromas of the growing onions and

garlic, basil, thyme, and rosemary. There were chickens clucking away around their coop, providing fresh eggs and fresh meat. The neighbors' lots were equally bountiful and always active. Water was pumped by hand from a well on the back porch. There was running water in the kitchen, but the novel cast-iron pump was a welcome companion as we made him spit water over his pouting bottom lip onto a colander of potatoes or onto our grass-stained feet.

The summertime was hot, with air that was thick and sweet. We would go down into the cellar for relief from the heat only to stand in awe of what must be described as a secret treasure: dozens of dusty mason jars filled with raspberry, strawberry, and rhubarb jams, pickled beets, pickled cucumbers, pickled cipollini onions, pickled green beans, and pickled radishes.

Grandma's hands were gnarled from arthritis and a lifetime of gardening, canning, sewing, mending, and living. Her stoic eyes reminded us that she had survived the Great Depression; an icy pale blue, deeply set, framed by well-worn creases over her nose and into her forehead, like a dried-up river or an old baseball glove. She made her dresses using inexpensive floral fabrics, which she wore with simple stockings and white tennis shoes. She had three pairs of the same shoes, purchased from the Sears catalog and worn categorically: one pair for gardening, one pair for cooking, and one pair for going to town. After washing the freshly picked strawber-

ries, she would cut them effortlessly with a paring knife against her callused thumb, never turning her eyes from our eager faces and watering mouths as she prepared breakfast.

Strawberries over peaches and cream. I picked the strawberries myself, and with the first taste my mouth woke up, followed quickly by my nose, as the fragrant, sweet, and earthy aromas widened my eyes. The peaches were next: ripe, soft, alive, and swimming in cream. Chewing and smiling at the same time, I enthusiastically nodded at my grandma to give my approval. She responded by handing me a cotton napkin.

To be honest, these memories had gone forgotten for some time. This might be because growing up in Iowa my thoughts were often focused on how to get out and head to the big city. I rarely took stock of where I came from—the sights, smells, and tastes that defined that place. But somehow those experiences stuck with me and shaped who I am and, more specifically, how I think about food. I learned that it isn't just the strawberry's fresh sweetness, the peach's soft texture, or the aroma of a freshly tempered chocolate bar—it is the details of its past, the impassioned love of its harvester, and the warmth of its surroundings that make it truly delicious. Recalling my early experiences offers a deeper understanding of the Mast Brothers' battle cry: "Make everything delicious!" —*RM*

CHOCOLATE MILK

Serves 4

Why is it that so many of us stop drinking chocolate milk as we grow older?
Homemade chocolate syrup (not powder) is the key to making this a timeless
(and ageless) beverage. Refrigerate leftover chocolate syrup.

CHOCOLATE SYRUP
(makes 2½ cups)

Water	2 cups
Sugar	½ cup
Cocoa powder	½ cup
Dark chocolate	1 ounce, chopped
Vanilla bean	Seeds scraped from ⅓ bean

CHOCOLATE MILK

Chocolate Syrup	1 cup (or to taste)
Whole milk	3 cups

Make the Chocolate Syrup
1. In a saucepan, mix water, sugar, cocoa powder, chocolate, and vanilla seeds and bring to a boil.
2. Take off heat, strain, and let cool.

Make the Chocolate Milk
3. Stir Chocolate Syrup into milk.

CLASSIC CHOCOLATE BROWNIES

Makes 16

///

Dark chocolate	12 ounces, chopped
Unsalted butter	¾ cup (1½ sticks)
Brown sugar	1¾ cups
Vanilla	2 teaspoons
Eggs	5
All-purpose flour	¾ cup
Baking powder	1 teaspoon
Sea salt	1 teaspoon
Almonds	½ cup chopped
Hazelnuts	½ cup chopped
Pecans	½ cup chopped

///

1. Preheat oven to 325 degrees Fahrenheit. Butter a 9-inch square baking pan.
2. Melt chocolate, butter, and brown sugar in a saucepan over low heat.
3. Add vanilla to mixture.
4. Add eggs and combine until smooth.
5. Add flour, baking powder, salt, and chopped nuts.
6. Mix until batter is well blended.
7. Pour into baking pan.
8. Bake for 30 minutes.
9. Let cool, and cut into 2-inch squares.

CHOCOLATE CHIP COOKIES

Makes 24

A timeless cookie for all ages and all seasons.
Don't forget to prepare a glass of chocolate milk.

/ /

Unsalted butter	1 cup (2 sticks), room temperature
Brown sugar	¾ cup
Granulated sugar	⅔ cup
Eggs	2
All-purpose flour	2¼ cups
Baking soda	1 teaspoon
Sea salt	1 teaspoon
Dark chocolate	15 ounces, chopped

/ /

1. Preheat oven to 350 degrees Fahrenheit.
2. In a large mixing bowl, cream softened butter with both sugars until fluffy.
3. Blend in eggs one at a time.
4. Add flour, baking soda, salt, and chocolate and combine.
5. Spoon cookie dough 2 inches apart onto a baking sheet using heaping tablespoons.
6. Bake for 15 minutes or until golden brown.

CHOCOLATE ICE CREAM

Makes 2 quarts

This stripped-down recipe really highlights the subtleties
and elegance of fine chocolate and home-churned ice cream.

Whole milk	4 cups
Heavy cream	1 cup
Sugar	¾ cup
Egg yolks	10
Dark chocolate	12 ounces, chopped

1. Combine milk and cream in a medium saucepan and bring to a boil.
2. In a medium bowl, combine sugar and egg yolks and whip until fluffy.
3. Combine both mixtures and heat to 180 degrees Fahrenheit. Test with an instant-read thermometer.
4. Add chocolate and stir until fully integrated. Let cool.
5. Churn according to instructions for your ice cream machine.

PEANUT BUTTER CUPS

Makes 24

Making your favorite candies from scratch is incredibly rewarding. You can ensure that only the best ingredients go into them, and the flavor will knock your socks off.

Smooth natural peanut butter	1 cup
Unsalted butter	4 tablespoons
Confectioners' sugar	1 cup
Sea salt	1 pinch
Dark chocolate	1 pound, melted and tempered (see page 9)

1. Melt peanut butter and butter in a saucepan over low heat.
2. Whisk in confectioners' sugar and salt and set aside.
3. Coat 24 mini muffin cups with tempered chocolate and refrigerate to set.
4. Once chocolate is set, fill cups with peanut butter filling.
5. Ladle remaining tempered chocolate over filling and refrigerate to set.

FINDING CHOCOLATE

Chocolate is arguably the most popular food in the world, and yet very few people know how it is made. How is it that we know so little about something we are all so familiar with and consume so often? This was the underlying question that drove us to commit our lives to making chocolate and to sharing our passion and educating our community. The idea of making chocolate from scratch arose one evening at a dinner party at our apartment in Williamsburg, Brooklyn. We didn't quite realize it at the time, but in asking a simple question, we had hit upon a revolutionary idea—handcrafting chocolate using nothing but cane sugar and cocoa beans with varying flavor profiles sourced from around the world.

Rick and I loved the prospect of starting a small business together, a family business. We were always competitive growing up, primarily in sports—basketball, baseball, soccer, and football—but were never afraid to share our ideas and dream big. We were both curious about how things were made, from backyard volcanoes to woodworking, furniture making, movies, and, of course, food. Growing up, we knew chocolate as a candy coated in lots of sugar. We certainly didn't treat chocolate like a food and never knew that chocolate was made from the fruits of trees.

Once off to college and then to our first jobs out of school, we landed on opposite coasts. But after eight years of living far from home and far from each other, our worlds were going to be coming back together. I moved to New York in the summer of 2001 with an economics degree, and struggled to find work. Paying the towering rents was difficult and eye-opening. I needed to cover bills and applied for an analyst job in finance; I was granted a second interview at Telligent Advisors in the World Trade Center on September 7, 2001. Sweating from nerves and wearing the baggy black suit I had bought in high school, I blew the interview and didn't get the job. Four days later, the attacks of 9/11 would level the Twin Towers, home to my would-be employer, and alter the world as we knew it.

For me, it was back to waiting tables and searching for internships. I crawled my way up, working in accounting for independent film-production companies. A year later, Rick, who had been working in music (everything from opera companies to record shops), started training in restaurant kitchens and decided to move to New York to pursue his new love affair with food. He crashed on the couch in my first apartment in Brooklyn, on Bartlett Street. The location was a mother's nightmare. Just south of the above-ground J-M-Z subway station, it was the only residential building on the block, nestled between vacant lots stamped with signs warning of toxic chemicals used to drive out the rats and a bus-repair shop that mainly operated after dark. There was no sink in the bathroom, and the sounds of cockfighting could be heard out the windows on occasion.

One night I heard a *POP!* and it suddenly looked as though somebody had turned on a spotlight outside. The windows were open, and smoke quickly started filling the apartment. I looked outside to see a car ablaze. Firefighters arrived thirty minutes later. We had a third roommate now, and looking around our cramped living quarters we unanimously decided to move. We found a place just fifteen blocks north, across from the Maujer Street Projects. It wasn't huge, but we each had our own bedroom; more important, there was space for a used butcher-block table that we had snagged for a hundred bucks. That table would be key in helping us to find chocolate.

Rick enrolled in and graduated from the Institute of Culinary Education, and followed that up with apprenticeships and work in New York City restaurant kitchens, including Gramercy Tavern and SoHo House, and our lives began to revolve around food. We made our own beer and breads and hosted dinner parties every Wednesday night, or whenever they would spontaneously erupt. Everyone would bring a dish to the table—meats from the local butcher, fish from the local market—and everything was homemade, from quiches and casseroles to pies and ice cream. Rick bought a roasting pan and loved cooking a whole leg of lamb after proudly marching down the street with it slung over his shoulder. I was not much of a cook but often acted as Rick's *sous chef*. My primary contribution was buying the wine. Lots of wine. Anyone and everyone was welcome, including neighbors in the building and from across the street.

The dinner parties would last late into the night and sometimes end at our local bar, the Bushwick Country Club. We'd become regulars there, spending long days grilling ribs in the backyard by the putt-putt golf course, which boasted a windmill made of Pabst Blue Ribbon cans. Joe and Bob McClure of McClure's Pickles were storing their canned pickles in the cellar. John Roberts, the bar owner, would offer us shots of whiskey chased with the pickle brine (coining the term *pickleback*) and would talk to us late into the night about what it's like to run a bar and own a business. We'd crawl out from under the closed gate at the end of the night, shielding our eyes from the rising sun.

Setting whiskey aside (but always within reach), we began making dessert, homemade ice cream, cakes, and pies. One evening, sitting around the table, we realized that none of us actually knew where chocolate came from or how it was made. How could that be? Again, it was arguably one of the most popular foods on earth, and yet nobody knew how chocolate was made. We knew how to buy it at the local grocery store and how to melt it to make truffles, cakes, and cookies, but after that our knowledge hit a wall. Clearly we needed to find out more.

Our heads were pounding the next day with the excitement of discovery on the horizon. We were going to figure out how to make chocolate. Chocolate came from pods that grew on the trunks of trees, and these pods were a fruit. Chocolate wasn't candy, we came to realize—it was *food*. The botanical name of the cacao tree, *Theobroma cacao*, translates as "food of the gods." We were hooked.

We read everything we could. We studied the unique varietals of cacao, the regions along the equator where it grows, the art of roasting, and the science of tempering; we dove into the vast, deep, rich history of cacao, a bean that was currency for the Aztecs and was turned into the first drinking chocolate by the Mayans. Rick even took a job at a *chocolaterie* in Manhattan. Although he saw that the finished creations took a great deal of skill, he was baffled that they were melting down chocolate bought in bulk from abroad. Remelting was commonplace for chocolatiers. To our amazement, barely a handful of companies were actually making chocolate from scratch in North America, and we were to be the first in New York in decades. This only strengthened our resolve and stirred our curiosity, ultimately encouraging us to make it on our own. We wanted to make chocolate from scratch. We set out to make the most delicious chocolate in the world. A pure chocolate, highlighting the unique characteristics of the beans that farmers worked so hard to harvest and ferment perfectly. A chocolate containing only two ingredients: cacao and cane sugar. We would create a product in a class of its own: American craft chocolate.
—*MM*

CHOCOLATE CUPCAKES

Makes 12

//

CUPCAKES

Unsalted butter	½ cup (1 stick)
Dark chocolate	2½ ounces, chopped
Sugar	¾ cup
Cocoa powder	½ cup
Eggs	2
All-purpose flour	¾ cup
Baking powder	¾ teaspoon
Baking soda	½ teaspoon
Sea salt	½ teaspoon
Heavy cream	1 cup

GANACHE

Heavy cream	1 cup
Dark chocolate	10 ounces, chopped

//

Make the Cupcakes

1. Preheat oven to 350 degrees Fahrenheit. Butter a 12-cup muffin tin or line with paper liners.
2. Melt butter and chocolate in a saucepan over low heat.
3. Add sugar and cocoa powder.
4. Mix in eggs and add flour, baking powder and soda, and salt.
5. Add heavy cream and combine.
6. Pour batter into muffin cups to fill halfway.
7. Bake for 15 minutes or until a toothpick inserted into the center comes out clean.

Make the Ganache

8. Bring cream to a boil in a saucepan.
9. Pour over chocolate in heatproof bowl and let sit for 2 minutes.
10. Stir until smooth.

Assemble

11. Spoon or pipe ganache over each cupcake.

CHOCOLATE MILK SHAKES

Serves 4

Make sure you serve these with both a straw and a spoon.
Thick and rich. Refrigerate the leftover chocolate syrup for another use.

CHOCOLATE SYRUP
(makes 2½ cups)

Water	2 cups
Sugar	½ cup
Cocoa powder	½ cup
Vanilla bean	Seeds scraped from ⅓ bean

MILK SHAKES

Good-quality store-bought vanilla ice cream	4 cups
Whole milk	2 cups
Chocolate Syrup	1 cup

Make the Chocolate Syrup

1. In a medium saucepan, mix water, sugar, cocoa powder, and vanilla and bring to a boil.
2. Take off heat, strain, and let cool.

Make the Milk Shakes

3. Combine ice cream, milk, and Chocolate Syrup in a blender.
4. Blend until smooth.

CHOCOLATE SODA

Serves 4

A refreshing homemade soda that can quench a thirst as well as feed a chocolate fix.
Refrigerate the leftover chocolate syrup for another use.

///////////////////////////////////////

CHOCOLATE SYRUP
(makes 2½ cups)

Water	2 cups
Sugar	½ cup
Cocoa powder	½ cup
Vanilla bean	Seeds scraped from ⅓ bean

SODA

Chocolate Syrup	2 cups
Seltzer	2 cups

///////////////////////////////////////

Make the Chocolate Syrup
1. In a medium saucepan, mix water, sugar, cocoa powder, and vanilla and bring to a boil.
2. Take off heat, strain, and let cool.

Make the Soda
3. Add Chocolate Syrup to seltzer and stir. Divide among tall glasses.

FROZEN CHOCOLATE POPS

Makes 4

Destined to become the new taste of summer.
Use this quick and easy recipe to keep your freezer stocked.

///

Whole milk	2¼ cups
Sugar	⅔ cup
Cocoa powder	¼ cup
Dark chocolate	7½ ounces, chopped, plus 10 ounces, melted and tempered (see page 9)

///

1. In a medium saucepan, combine milk, sugar, and cocoa powder and bring to a boil.
2. Pour liquid over chopped chocolate in a bowl and let sit for 2 minutes.
3. Stir until emulsified.
4. Pour into ice-pop molds and freeze.
5. Dip frozen pops in tempered chocolate.
6. Put into freezer to set.

CHOCOLATE PUDDING

Serves 8

//

Cocoa powder	2 tablespoons
Cornstarch	2 tablespoons
Sea salt	¼ teaspoon
Whole milk	2¼ cups
Vanilla	1 teaspoon
Egg yolks	2
Egg	1
Sugar	6 tablespoons
Unsalted butter	2 tablespoons
Dark chocolate	5 ounces, chopped

//

1. Mix cocoa powder, cornstarch, and salt in a bowl.
2. In a medium saucepan, combine milk and vanilla and bring to a boil. Take off heat.
3. In a medium bowl, mix egg yolks with egg and sugar and whisk until fluffy.
4. Incorporate all three mixtures together in the saucepan.
5. Cook over medium heat, stirring constantly, until thickened.
6. Add butter and chocolate and mix until smooth and shiny.
7. Pour pudding into small bowls or ramekins.
8. Let cool in refrigerator for 2 hours before serving.

DOUBLE CHOCOLATE CHIP COOKIES

Makes 24

This is the perfect recipe for when a regular chocolate chip cookie just won't cut it.

///

Unsalted butter	½ cup (1 stick), room temperature
Sugar	1⅔ cups
Maple syrup	4½ teaspoons
Eggs	4
All-purpose flour	½ cup
Baking powder	1 tablespoon
Sea salt	1 teaspoon
Dark chocolate chips	8 ounces
Dark chocolate	8 ounces, melted

///

1. Preheat oven to 350 degrees Fahrenheit.
2. In a medium bowl using a handheld mixer, combine butter with sugar and maple syrup.
3. Add eggs one at a time, making sure they are fully incorporated each time.
4. Add flour, baking powder, salt, chocolate chips, and melted chocolate and mix to form dough.
5. Spoon the cookie dough 2 inches apart onto a baking sheet using heaping tablespoons.
6. Bake for 15 minutes.

– Part Two –

SOURCING & GATHERING

ORGANIC CACAO
OF BELIZE
Moho River Cacao
PRODUCED BY:
MOHO RIVER CACAO, LT
TOLEDO, BELIZE
CERTIFIED ORGANIC BY

A CACAO FARMER

The small hand-painted sign that greets us at the end of our drive through the rolling and rugged dirt roads just outside the Mayan village of San Pedro Columbia in Belize reads, simply, "Welcome to Agouti Cacao Farm, owned by Eladio Pop." To the average westerner, there is nothing farm-like about Eladio's farm. There are no fences or rows of planted cacao trees, no large equipment or trucks, no barns or farm animals, just a perfect narrow path that winds up and down the hilly terrain. But even more unusual than the jungle farm is the farmer. Mud boots on, machete in hand, and a headband made of sugarcane, Eladio Pop, of Mopan Mayan descent, is unlike any farmer we've ever encountered. With passion and a big, bright smile, Eladio shares his land and story.

The cacao tree, *Theobroma cacao*, grows best with overhead shade, and there is no shortage of shade in this most biodynamic farm. There are banana trees with fruit that tastes like apples, which rejuvenate us during our hike, and other exotic fruit trees, including mango, coconut, and lime. There is also towering jipijapa, which locals have coined the "tourist tree" because its bark turns red and peels away like sunburned skin. Eladio has been working on this land since he was a teenager and vows never to neglect the earth that he is a part of and which is now a part of him. His organic farming methods guide the natural cycles that his jungle already possesses. He doesn't use any pesticides or herbicides. With his machete, he weeds, prunes, and thins the canopy, allowing the sun to shower the young plants, and then grows the proper seedlings next to those that need shade.

Eladio's cacao is scattered throughout the jungle and ranges from the new seedlings he plants each year to trees that are more than 100 years old, which can still produce fruit using grafting methods. The pods, which grow primarily on the trunks of the trees and look like a small football, have orange, red, green, purple, and yellow skins, which give off a glow in the jungle. Once they are ready to be harvested, Eladio gently cuts the pods at the stem with his machete and gathers them in piles. These pods will soon be cut open, the pulp and seeds removed to undergo fermentation in wooden boxes covered with banana leaves. After five to seven days, the cacao will be laid out to dry under the sun for another ten days or so, depending on the weather conditions. He tells us that cacao is what gives him life, strength, and energy. We cut open a few pods to taste the sweet and citrusy pulp that surrounds the freshly exposed cacao seeds.

We continue hiking and harvesting cacao through the jungle, pausing often to stop and taste or smell freshly cut sugarcane, allspice leaves, wild ginger, and dragonfruit. Eladio is a proud father of this land, and he doesn't hesitate to share its offerings. We will not walk away hungry. As we reach the top of the hills, he stops again to express thanks for what the land has given him, as he in turn protects the farm and these Mayan mountains for his ancestors and for future generations. He's planted new trees that will remind his grandchildren and their grandchildren of his work and love of the land, as the trees will grow to be tall in the next thirty years, dotting the landscape and lining the hillsides with their peaceful pink flowers. We take a break on a hammock in the shade, where he shows us the worn Bible he used to teach himself how to read. He offers another treat for our palates, this time honeycomb made in a teakettle swarmed with bees.

After taking in the views from the mountaintop, and with the taste of sweet nectar on our tongues, we head back down to join Eladio's wife, Virginia, who is awaiting our arrival to make us a traditional Mayan drinking chocolate. Eladio's house is built of cement, with open windows and doors keeping it airy and cool and an attached back patio used to dry the cocoa beans. Virginia and their daughter Adalia, wearing vibrant fuchsia dresses that they made, are roasting cocoa beans over an open fire. The aromas fill the outdoor patio and waft out into the valley of Hobbit-like homes belonging to the neighbors and villagers below. Using a stone to crack the beans, they are left with a mixture of nibs and shells. Adalia gently but sharply rocks the mixture in a rosewood bowl, tossing the contents into the air, allowing the wind to blow away the undesirable husks while preserving the denser nibs. This is a traditional method of winnowing mastered by the Mayans. Left with just the nibs, she takes a granite stone and rhythmically crushes them, along with cane sugar and allspice, on a stone *metate* that has been in the family for generations.

The chocolate begins to form and we roll it with our fingers, place it in the hand-carved drinking bowls, add the hot water, and enjoy Eladio's favorite elixir. He tells us that it's drinking chocolate that gives him strength and energy, not to mention fifteen children. Yes, fifteen. They range just over thirty years from youngest to oldest, and, even more impressively, all from his one and only loving wife, who has been pregnant for most of her adult life.

Eladio and Virginia even began feeding their children the liquid surrounding the cacao seeds when the children were just one week old, and he has been drinking it since he was a small child. He tells us he drinks at least six cups a day. "This seed is something really special for your heart. If I don't drink it for the day, it's like something is missing. When I drink cacao, my heart is happy." —*MM*

MAYAN HOT CHOCOLATE

Serves 4

This is how chocolate was consumed for hundreds of years.

///

Water	2 cups
Honey	2 tablespoons
Ground allspice	1 teaspoon
Whole cinnamon	1 stick
Vanilla bean	Seeds scraped from ½ bean
Dark chocolate	2½ ounces, chopped

///

1. In a saucepan, bring water with honey, allspice, cinnamon, and vanilla to a boil.
2. Pour hot water mixture over chocolate in a clean saucepan.
3. Mix to emulsify.
4. Strain and serve.

DRINKING CHOCOLATE

Serves 4

Thick, velvety texture with rich, deep chocolate flavor. This simple application really
highlights the unique characteristics of various cacao origins. Madagascar will provide
a nice hint of citrus; Ecuador will provide notes of cinnamon.

//

Whole milk	2 cups
Sugar	2 tablespoons
Dark chocolate	5 ounces, finely chopped

//

1. In a saucepan, bring milk and sugar to a boil.
2. Pour hot milk mixture over chopped chocolate in a bowl.
3. Mix until smooth, and serve immediately.

MOLE SAUCE

Serves 8

Mole poblano is probably the most common variety of mole. The recipe we have provided here is a
bit darker, more like a mole Oaxaca. The photo shows three beautiful variations on the recipe.
Mole sauces can be the ultimate expression of locavorism. No two moles are alike, so use our recipe
as a starting point and be creative with the dried chiles and other spices, putting your own
localized stamp on this Mexican favorite. It's most commonly served with chicken.

Mulato chiles	8
Ancho chiles	6
Pasilla chiles	6
Chipotle chile	1
Sesame seeds	½ cup, plus 1 teaspoon for garnish
Black peppercorns	½ teaspoon
Dried thyme	½ teaspoon
Ground cinnamon	½ teaspoon
Whole cloves	¼ teaspoon
Lard	1 tablespoon
Raisins	¼ cup
Almonds	¼ cup
Pecans	¼ cup
Corn tortilla	1, torn into pieces
Garlic	4 cloves, minced
Onion	½, chopped
Tomatoes	1 pound, chopped
Tomatillos	3, husked, rinsed, and roughly chopped
Banana	½, sliced
Chicken broth	10 cups
Dark chocolate	5 ounces, chopped
Sea salt	1 tablespoon

1. In a bowl, cover all chile peppers with hot water. Let stand for 30 minutes.

2. In a cast-iron skillet, combine ½ cup sesame seeds, peppercorns, thyme, cinnamon, and cloves. Toast over low heat, stirring, for about 2 minutes.

3. Let spices cool. Grind in a spice grinder to a powder and set aside.

4. In the same skillet, melt the lard.

5. Add raisins, almonds, pecans, and tortilla to skillet and cook on low heat until almonds are browned and raisins are plump. Transfer mixture to a bowl.

6. Add the garlic, onion, tomatoes, tomatillos, banana, and spice powder to the skillet and cook over moderately high heat for about 8 minutes. Transfer to the bowl and let cool.

7. Drain the chiles.

8. Add chiles and chicken broth to the bowl. Transfer to an earthenware or cast-iron pot, cover partially, and simmer for 1 hour.

9. Transfer sauce to a food processor, add chocolate, and purée.

10. Add salt.

11. Toast remaining teaspoon of sesame seeds to use as garnish.

CLASSIC HOT COCOA

Serves 4

Serve piping hot with a toasted marshmallow.

/ /

Whole milk	4 cups
Cocoa powder	¼ cup
Brown sugar	¼ cup
Vanilla	1 teaspoon
Dark chocolate	2 ounces

/ /

1. In a medium saucepan, combine milk, cocoa powder, sugar, and vanilla.
2. Bring to a boil, stirring frequently.
3. Shave chocolate over each mug.

THE MAINE COAST

"We are tied to the ocean. And when we go back to the sea, whether it is to sail or to watch—we are going back from whence we came."
—John. F. Kennedy

⁄ ⁄ ⁄ ⁄ ⁄ ⁄ ⁄

*T*he entire Northeast has been going through a heat wave. It's the week of the Fourth of July and the weather is horribly humid and in the upper nineties, so we have the air-conditioning blowing through our Volvo station wagon, which we named Olive because of the color and my wife Natasha's love of anthropomorphism. Natasha sits comfortably in the back seat with our son, Sebastian, who has just turned one year old and has taken to his car seat nicely, even on long trips. I drive with a proud smile on my face, as I am finally taking my family on our first vacation.

For a few months prior to the trip, my wife and I had been doing research as to where in Maine we were going to go. Kennebunkport? Portland? Camden? Acadia? After putting our son to bed, we had spent many a late night flipping through online photos, room rates, and maps, trying to settle on the perfect little cabin (given our tight budget) to get away from it all.

My wife and I had finally booked a small cottage just north of the famed Nubble Lighthouse on York Beach. The beach was not too far from home and was ranked as one of the best family vacation spots in the country. Perfect.

Having grown up without a father, but deeply determined to be the best one ever, I find myself saying outrageously cheesy dad things like, "Take in that sea air, guys, it's just what the doctor ordered," and stating obvious facts as though I've been spending summers in Maine my whole life. Looking back in the rearview mirror, my smile flattens a bit as I see my wife, bare feet on the headrest in front of her and deep into the latest Kathy Reichs novel, with my son fast asleep next to her. I look forward, smile, slowly shake my head, and mutter something I had thought dads should say, like, "People just don't appreciate the journey." I am fated to be the most embarrassing father to my son.

As we cross the Piscataqua River from New Hampshire to Maine, we are eager to turn off the air-conditioning, roll down the windows, and let the healing Maine air flow through our lungs. Drawing deep breaths through my nose, I can already smell and taste the salt, that most precious of minerals and an ingredient that we are very much in love with. Mast Brothers Chocolate has sourced its salt for many years now from the coast of Maine, where Stephen Cook and his wife, Sharon, set the standard for American saltworks at the Maine Sea Salt Company.

Driving north past Lobster Bay on Highway 1A, we see the ocean open up to the east to an extensive run of beach. The traffic slows as vacationers run back and forth over the road to their cottages or to grab a lobster roll at one of the many shacks. The familiar Nubble Light sits modestly at the end of the rocks. We continue on to Main Street and pull into the driveway of a beautiful inn. Here rocking chairs line the expansive front porch overlooking the ocean, and a brass band sets up inside a gazebo for the evening performance and community dance. Behind this historic inn is a teeny-tiny cottage. *Our* cottage. A one-bedroom shingled hut (that would make a New York one-bedroom look like a penthouse) with a yellow kitchenette, wood paneling, polyester curtains with lace fringe, mismatched plaid linens, fake flowers, and a small front porch. To my wife and me, it is a palace by the sea.

Or so we thought.

There is something about the first twenty-four hours of a family vacation with an exhausted wife and a teething child that is difficult to explain. I'll call it the transitional period, when the manic, frenzied, "normal" way of life must be eroded away by the waves and salty wind. And this takes time. During the first day, I don't think there was a single word that either of us said that didn't drive the other crazy. Every decision, no matter how trivial, churned our faces with gnarled tension and furled lips. When should we go to the beach? What do you want for lunch? Where are the towels? Is the car locked? All seemed to invite scowls, sighs, and eye rolls. It was obviously time to eat.

Lobster guacamole, lobster rolls, more lobster rolls. Lobster burritos, lobster pizza, lobster mac and cheese. Half lobsters, whole lobsters, lobster tails, and lobster bisque. Would you like your Caesar salad with or without lobster? Saltwater taffy by the ton, bacon-caramel kettle corn by the bag, and chocolate fudge on every corner. Unable to do anything in moderation, I ate and loved it all. While dipping claws into ramekins of butter, I imagined life as a lobster fisherman. That was Stephen Cook's life prior to starting the Maine Sea Salt Company. Bringing the sea's bounty to his community's dinner table gave him great pride and a sense of purpose. Realizing that he could fulfill this mission in a unique way and make an even greater impact, he began building solar houses to harvest the salt directly from his beloved coast.

By the end of the second day, we were ready to submit to relaxation. Our cottage was literally across the street from Short Sands Beach, a beautiful family-friendly stretch of soft, wet sand with wickedly cold water. It was so cold that it took days before I fully immersed. When I finally did, it changed my life like a baptism. I rose from the water laughing uncontrollably and basically speaking in tongues. I darted my eyes to the other believers as if to say, "I get it now!"

There were families everywhere. It was an incredible feeling of camaraderie to join in ocean-side conversations with other fathers, children running free around us, telling me how lucky I was with Sebastian's tempera-ment. Joking about how I'd better brush up on my baseball knowledge and skills. Talking trash about the Yankees and wondering if I'd be cheering for the Brooklyn Nets or the Knicks.

On the fourth day, the three of us discovered candlepin bowling, and it was love at first sight. I say "discovered" because we found the bowling alley, abandoned by the tourists and hidden behind racks of Maine sweatshirts, boogie boards, and umbrellas, in an oversize warehouse building with a sign that said "Fun O Rama." The long, thin, wooden alley planks had a weathered patina and were no doubt in need of repair, but I loved it just how it was. The small bocce-size balls had been slammed against the pins hundreds of thousands of times, and it showed. I quickly set out to master this game. From my first toss I tried some nice right-to-left spin on the ball, taking detailed mental notes on my breathing and footwork. "Continuous improvement, Rick," I said under my breath, with clenched jaw. "What did you just say?" my wife asked with an astonished laugh. I gave her a mischievous smile to let her know that I wasn't taking everything too seriously. Every day from then on, we had breakfast and headed to the bowling alley for a game or two, and back again after dinner, just before sunset.

The vacationers on York Beach are different from those in Williamsburg, Brooklyn. The men are fathers and firemen, not graphic designers. They proudly offer up their arms and legs, not for tattoos but for use as a jungle gym by their children. They happily engage in conversation with their aging parents. Goatees outnumber beards, and the vacationers in Maine sport Red Sox hats and Patriots shirts rather than Brooklyn Nets hats and American Apparel. Don't get me wrong; I love Brooklyn more than any place in the world, but I also loved being in a community that centered on family and sharing. Maine shares its incredible coast by opening its arms to desperate souls who are overworked and overstressed. The saltwater air and the ocean itself heal, transport, and soothe. And thanks to the Cook family, Maine sea salt has been bottled for all to enjoy. —*RM*

CHOCOLATE BLUEBERRY PIE

Serves 8

The wild blueberry is the official fruit of Maine. Pick fresh blueberries as early
as May and as late as August. If you can't make it to Maine, look for wild blueberries
at your local farmers' market or fine-foods store.

//

CRUST

All-purpose flour	1⅓ cups
Cocoa powder	6 tablespoons
Sea salt	1 teaspoon
Unsalted butter	¾ cup (1½ sticks), room temperature
Confectioners' sugar	¼ cup
Egg yolk	1
Heavy cream	1½ teaspoons

FILLING

Fresh wild blueberries	5 cups
Dark chocolate	2 ounces, chopped, plus more for shaving
Sugar	1 cup
Cornstarch	4 tablespoons

//

Make the Crust

1. Preheat oven to 350 degrees Fahrenheit. Butter an 8-inch pie plate.
2. Combine flour, cocoa powder, and salt in a medium bowl.
3. In the bowl of a standing mixer, cream butter and confectioners' sugar and add dry ingredients.
4. Add egg yolk and cream, and mix to form dough.
5. Refrigerate dough for 30 minutes.
6. Roll dough ⅛ inch thick, poke fork holes, and set in the pie plate.

Make the Filling and Bake

7. Toss and lightly crush blueberries with chopped chocolate, sugar, and cornstarch until well combined.
8. Pour blueberry mixture over dough in the pie plate.
9. Bake for 45 minutes.
10. Shave chocolate over blueberry filling.

CHOCOLATE TURTLES

Makes 12

This classic confection gets its name from its turtle-like shape.

Pecans	1 cup, quartered
Sugar	1 cup
Heavy cream	1 cup
Unsalted butter	1 tablespoon
Dark chocolate	1 pound, melted and tempered (see page 9)

---

1. Preheat oven to 350 degrees Fahrenheit.

2. Place pecans on baking sheet and bake for 12 minutes.

3. Melt sugar in a shallow pan and cook over medium heat until amber brown.

4. Carefully combine cream with sugar and butter, stirring vigorously with a fork.

5. Bring caramel mixture to 240 degrees Fahrenheit (check with an instant-read thermometer) and add pecans.

6. Spoon large coin-size portions of mixture onto a baking sheet.

7. Once cooled, dip in tempered chocolate.

CHOCOLATE FUDGE

Makes 24 pieces

When we were growing up in Iowa, the first week of December always found
our mom making her famous chocolate fudge and gifting it door to door.

Heavy cream	1/3 cup
Whole milk	1/3 cup
Sugar	1¾ cups
Sea salt	1 teaspoon
Dark chocolate	2½ ounces, chopped
Vanilla	1 teaspoon
Unsalted butter	2 tablespoons, cut into small cubes

1. Combine cream, milk, sugar, salt, chocolate, and vanilla in a medium saucepan.
2. Over medium heat, slowly bring to a boil. Boil for 5 minutes.
3. Add butter cubes but do not stir.
4. Let cool to room temperature. Mix with a wooden spoon.
5. Pour into a 9-inch square baking pan and let cool.
6. Cut into small squares.

CHOCOLATE SAUCE

Makes 1 pint

The simplicity of this recipe demands great chocolate. No vanilla, no corn syrup
to mask poor ingredients, so get the best! Serve warm over ice cream.

Heavy cream	1½ cups
Sugar	1 tablespoon
Dark chocolate	5 ounces, chopped

1. In a saucepan, bring cream and sugar to a boil.
2. Pour over chopped chocolate in a heatproof bowl and let melt.
3. Using a spatula, stir in tight circles to emulsify.

CHOCOLATE PEANUT BUTTER COOKIES

Makes 24

Ever make your own peanut butter? Why not give it a try today? Just grab some peanuts, a little sugar, salt, and a food processor. Homemade PB makes these cookies even tastier.

Unsalted butter	1 cup (2 sticks), room temperature
Brown sugar	2 cups
Eggs	2
All-purpose flour	1½ cups
Cocoa powder	⅔ cup
Baking soda	2 teaspoons
Dark chocolate	5 ounces, finely chopped
Peanuts	2 cups, chopped
Peanut butter	1 cup

1. Preheat oven to 350 degrees Fahrenheit.
2. In a large bowl, cream butter with brown sugar and eggs.
3. Add flour, cocoa powder, and baking soda and combine.
4. Add chocolate, peanuts, and peanut butter and combine.
5. Scoop tablespoon-size balls of dough onto a baking sheet.
6. Bake for 12 minutes.

WHOOPIE PIES

Makes 12

This dessert originates from the Amish farms of Maine and Pennsylvania.
When the farmers would break for lunch and find this chocolate treat in their lunch pail,
legend has it, they would shout "Whoopie!"

///

CAKES

Unsalted butter	½ cup (1 stick), room temperature
Brown sugar	1 cup
Eggs	2
All-purpose flour	2½ cups
Cocoa powder	½ cup
Sea salt	1 teaspoon
Baking powder	1 teaspoon
Baking soda	½ teaspoon
Whole milk	1 cup

CREAM CHEESE FILLING

Cream cheese	8 ounces
Vanilla bean	Seeds scraped from ½ bean
Heavy cream	¼ cup
Confectioners' sugar	¼ cup

///

Make the Cakes
1. Preheat oven to 350 degrees Fahrenheit.
2. In the bowl of a standing mixer, cream butter and brown sugar until fluffy.
3. Add eggs one at a time and combine.
4. Add flour, cocoa powder, salt, and baking powder and soda and combine.
5. Add milk and mix until incorporated.
6. Spoon batter in 3-inch cakes onto a baking sheet.
7. Bake cakes for 14 minutes. Let cool.

Make the Filling
8. In the clean bowl of the standing mixer, whip cream cheese with vanilla bean.
9. Add heavy cream and sugar. Beat until combined.
10. Sandwich filling between cakes. Whoopie!

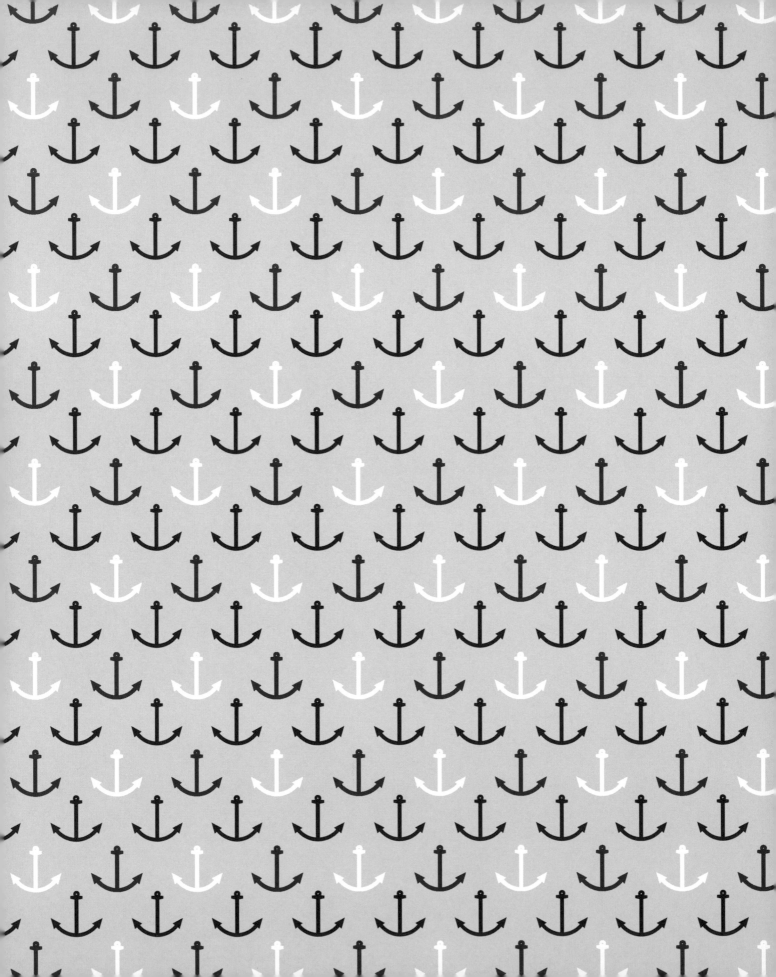

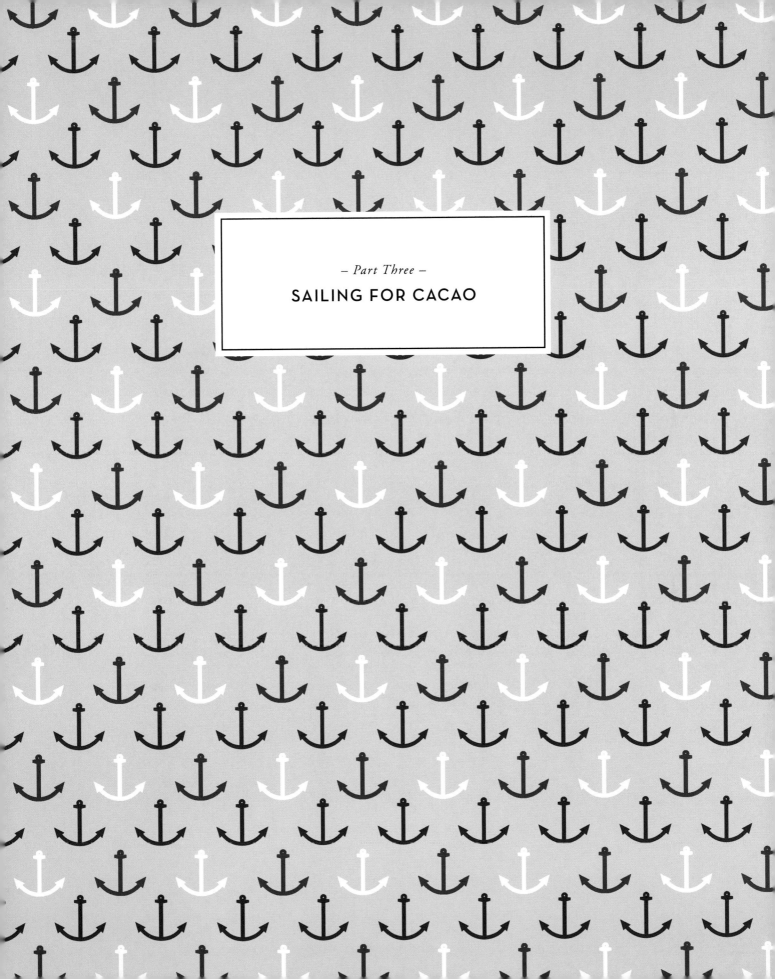

– Part Three –

SAILING FOR CACAO

FINDING A BOAT

"If Columbus had an advisory committee he would probably still be at the dock."
—*Arthur J. Goldberg*

⁄ ⁄ ⁄ ⁄ ⁄ ⁄ ⁄ ⁄

*A*s I stepped over the hand-carved wooden railing of the ship, I was greeted by Scooby, a full-grown Great Dane the color of weathered cedar shingles with the temperament of a kind and curious puppy. His owner was the captain and the builder of the seventy-foot schooner I had just boarded and the man I had been waiting to meet for over a year. Captain Eric Loftfield was in his fifties, wore a white beard, wind-worn skin, and a Carhartt jacket that looked like it may have been a high-school graduation gift, worn, ripping apart, sun-bleached, and stained with dirt, grease, and paint. "Only politicians wear a new working jacket," he would say. His boat shoes followed suit, worn and loved, and he wore a hand-sewn wool bicycle cap with a small brim. It was as if he had been cast for the role of sailor, but the focus and the experience in his eyes were real, his reassuring smile and demeanor were real. This was the type of reassurance that I was looking for if he was going to be the one to sail us and more than $100,000 worth of cargo from the Dominican Republic to Brooklyn.

But I've gotten ahead of myself.

It was the beginning of 2008 and Mast Brothers Chocolate was just starting to take form. Already there was a lot of interest in what we were doing, as we were one of the only true craft chocolate makers in the country and we were very much a part of the fast-growing and much-hyped Brooklyn locavore scene. Although my brother and I were the first local producers of chocolate in New York City for many decades, we often would smirk about how there is very little that is local

in terms of ingredient sourcing. Cacao is grown around the world, but the trees are found only near the equator. And cane sugar—well, that doesn't grow in Brooklyn either.

After a long day of sorting, roasting, winnowing, grinding, and tempering, Michael and I ran to the nearest wine shop and picked up a bottle or three to bring back to the factory to enjoy while we finished cleaning up, in constant chatter about what was on the horizon. Our discussions began with practicality, function, and innocence and soon drifted into brotherly wrangling over who does more work around the shop. "Could you make sure to e-mail Joe back about the tempering machines, Mike?" After another glass of wine the conversation transitioned into utopian soapboxing about how we would reinvent the modern family business.

On this particular day, I was going on and on (as I often do) about the glories and virtues of simplicity. *Simplify* had become a call to arms, and I wanted to apply it to how we shipped and received our beans.

"Let's just sail them," I said casually, perhaps to stir my brother's attention and get a rise out of him rather than as an actual business proposal.

Surprisingly, my brother didn't cut me off or roll his eyes. Maybe we are onto something here, I thought to myself. It's arguable as to whether or not Michael enjoys his role as sounding board and idea filter, but in this circumstance he patiently heard me out, and I began to take my own suggestion more seriously.

"So it's settled—we will set sail within three years. Planning begins now." With a look of nervous optimism and a weary smile, Michael raised his glass. "Why the hell not? Let's do it."

The following day I awoke energized and eager to share the news of our momentous decision. All my life it has been a deliberate strategy of mine to tell as many people as I can what I want to do. It gives me the often-needed motivation to complete a task. I can't say that it is the most endearing way to go about getting things done; in fact, I know it annoys the hell out of my brother, and my mother even more so, but I find great energy in it. Bold ideas put out into the world have a way of drawing others out of the woodwork to help make them happen. I was so excited to tell everyone at the shop (not to mention everyone at the bodega, the coffee shop, and everyone I passed on the street) that we were going to set sail, collect a large shipment of cacao, and sail it back using no oil, just the power of wind. Impractical? Not cost-effective? Wind is free!

Now all we needed to do was find a boat.

Months, maybe years, later, we were looking to hire another chocolate maker and were accepting resumes. Early one morning I was checking e-mail (something that I try to do as infrequently as possible) and stumbled upon an inquiry from Conor Hagen. He was working for a small Vermont chocolatier, mentioned significant sailing experience, and had a degree in film. He had no idea about our sailing ambitions. We hired him immediately.

On Conor's first day of work, there was a blizzard. The two of us spent most of the morning shoveling the front sidewalk together, and I described to him our seaward plans. Conor is even-tempered, but I could tell he was taken with the idea. I told him that little did he know but his sailing experience, in part, got him the job—and who knows, maybe in a few years he'd be out to sea.

After settling into the chocolate-making routine at our factory, we began getting more serious about putting a plan in motion to set sail. We set up a meeting with Conor, as we needed all the help we could get tracking down a boat. From our months of research, we had only heard of one converted fishing vessel that was capable of sailing cargo, and it was docked in Hawaii. As luck would have it, Conor's father had spoken to a captain by the name of Lu Yoder on Martha's Vineyard, who had heard of a captain and boat builder in Falmouth who'd been working on a sailing cargo vessel in his yard for decades, and Yoder would be happy to put us in touch.

Within a few weeks, we were planning our first trip out to Cape Cod to meet the captain. We couldn't believe our luck.

With Conor at the wheel, the three of us made our way to Cape Cod. The captain and boat builder had already become a man of legend to us. We arrived at the Kingman Yacht Center, parked the car, and nervously walked to the docks. Off in the distance we could see what appeared to be a giant pirate ship. Hauntingly black with three soaring masts, the *Black Seal* was the ship farthest out in the water. It miniaturized the rest of the boats there. We hopped in a motorboat and weaved our way around fishing boats, yachts, and day cruisers. We circled the ship, taking it all in, Captain Eric waving at us from the deck. Our adventure had begun. —*RM*

CHOCOLATE MARBLE CAKE

Serves 8

Top this cake with a rich ganache (see page 31)
or a simple dusting of confectioners' sugar.

//

YELLOW CAKE

Eggs	2
Egg yolk	1
Buttermilk	¾ cup
Unsalted butter	½ cup (1 stick), room temperature
Cake flour	1½ cups
Sugar	1 cup
Baking powder	2 teaspoons
Sea salt	½ teaspoon

CHOCOLATE CAKE

Egg	1
Egg yolk	1
Buttermilk	¾ cup
Unsalted butter	½ cup (1 stick), room temperature
Cake flour	1 cup
Sugar	1 cup
Cocoa powder	½ cup
Baking soda	1 teaspoon
Sea salt	¼ teaspoon

//

Make the Yellow Cake

1. Preheat oven to 350 degrees Fahrenheit. Butter and flour a 9-inch round cake pan.

2. Whisk together eggs, egg yolk, and half of the buttermilk.

3. In a separate bowl, using a whisk or a handheld mixer, blend butter with flour, sugar, baking powder, and salt until smooth.

4. Combine both mixtures and add remaining buttermilk.

Make the Chocolate Cake

5. Whisk together egg, yolk, and half of the buttermilk.

6. In a separate bowl, using a whisk or a handheld mixer, blend butter with flour, sugar, cocoa powder, baking soda, and salt until smooth.

7. Combine both mixtures and add remaining buttermilk.

Finish

8. Spoon batters into cake pan and gently swirl for marbling effect.

9. Bake for 45 minutes.

CHOCOLATE BOURBON BALLS

Makes 24 balls

Don't forget to test the bourbon extensively for flavor before,
during, and after preparation.

Vanilla wafer cookies	4 cups
Pecans	1 cup
Confectioners' sugar	1 cup
Cocoa powder	1 tablespoon
Bourbon	½ cup

1. Mix cookies, pecans, ¾ cup confectioners' sugar, and cocoa powder in a food processor.
2. Add bourbon and combine.
3. Roll mixture into small balls.
4. Roll balls in remaining confectioners' sugar to coat.

BOSTON CREAM PIE

Serves 10

This "pie" was invented in Boston in the 1850s at the Parker House Hotel.

///////////////////////////////////////

SPONGE CAKE

Eggs	8
Granulated sugar	2 cups
Cake flour	2 cups
Baking powder	1 tablespoon

PASTRY CREAM

Whole milk	4 cups
Vanilla bean	Seeds scraped from 1 bean
Egg yolks	4
Eggs	2
Granulated sugar	2 cups
Cornstarch	½ cup
Unsalted butter	¼ cup (½ stick)

CHOCOLATE GLAZE

Dark chocolate	4 ounces, chopped
Unsalted butter	¼ cup (½ stick)
Confectioners' sugar	2 cups
Hot water	½ cup

///////////////////////////////////////

Make the Sponge Cake

1. Preheat oven to 375 degrees Fahrenheit. Butter and flour a 12-inch round cake pan.
2. Whisk eggs and sugar together until thickened.
3. Combine and sift the flour and baking powder and fold into egg mixture.
4. Pour into cake pan.
5. Bake for 40 minutes. Let cool.

Make the Pastry Cream

6. Combine milk and vanilla seeds in a medium saucepan and bring to a boil.
7. Beat egg yolks, eggs, and half of the granulated sugar until fluffy.
8. Add cornstarch and remaining sugar to yolk mixture and combine.
9. Add the hot milk and whisk constantly over medium heat until thick.
10. Stir in the butter and let cool.

Make the Chocolate Glaze

11. Melt chocolate and butter in a double boiler.
12. Add confectioners' sugar and hot water to melted chocolate.
13. Mix until emulsified and smooth.

Assemble

14. Cut cooled sponge cake in half horizontally.
15. Spread pastry cream on top of one half.
16. Layer remaining cake half on top of pastry cream.
17. Spread chocolate glaze over top of cake.

CHOCOLATE-COVERED PRETZELS

Makes 12

///

DOUGH

Lukewarm water	1½ cups
Instant yeast	1 package
Sugar	1 tablespoon
Sea salt	2 teaspoons
All-purpose flour	4 cups
Unsalted butter	4 tablespoons, room temperature

COOKING LIQUID

Water	10 cups
Baking soda	⅔ cup

EGG WASH

Egg yolks	2
Water	1 tablespoon

CHOCOLATE GARNISH

Dark chocolate	8 ounces, melted and tempered (see page 9)
Sea salt	4 tablespoons

///

Make the Dough

1. Combine lukewarm water (110–115 degrees Fahrenheit) with instant yeast, sugar, and salt.

2. Let sit for 10 minutes or until the mixture begins to foam.

3. In a standing mixer, using the dough paddle, add flour and butter, kneading the dough for ten minutes.

4. Cover dough and let sit in warm place for 1 hour or until dough has risen to double its size.

Shape and Cook the Pretzels

5. Preheat oven to 450 degrees Fahrenheit.

6. Combine 10 cups water and baking soda. Bring to a boil.

7. Divide dough into 12 equal pieces.

8. Roll each piece into a 20-inch rope.

9. Make U shape with the rope, holding the ends.

10. Cross ends over each other, pinching ends onto bottom of dough.

11. Place pretzels into boiling water, one by one, for 30 seconds.

12. Place boiled pretzels onto parchment-lined baking sheet.

13. Combine egg yolks with 1 tablespoon water. Brush pretzels with egg wash.

14. Place in oven and bake for 15 minutes.

15. Transfer to a cooling rack. Cool completely.

16. Dip pretzels in tempered chocolate and sprinkle on salt.

CHOCOLATE GINGERSNAPS

Makes 24

There is nothing like the aroma that surrounds you when these are first pulled from the oven.
The fresh spice of ginger with rich craft chocolate is the perfect combination.

Unsalted butter	½ cup (1 stick), room temperature
Brown sugar	½ cup
Molasses	¼ cup
Water	2 teaspoons
Fresh ginger	3 tablespoons grated
All-purpose flour	1½ cups
Cocoa powder	1 tablespoon
Baking soda	1 teaspoon
Ground ginger	1 teaspoon
Ground cinnamon	1 teaspoon
Ground nutmeg	½ teaspoon
Dark chocolate	7½ ounces, chopped
Granulated sugar	1 cup

1. In the bowl of a standing mixer, cream butter with brown sugar until fluffy.
2. Add molasses, water, and fresh ginger and combine.
3. Add flour, cocoa powder, baking soda, ground ginger, cinnamon, and nutmeg and combine.
4. Add chocolate and mix just enough to blend into a dough.
5. Wrap dough in plastic and refrigerate for 2 hours.
6. Preheat oven to 350 degrees Fahrenheit.
7. Shape the dough into 1½-inch balls and roll them in granulated sugar.
8. Place cookies on a baking sheet and bake for 14 minutes. Remove from oven and
bask in the aroma, but let cool before devouring.

CACAO NIB SCALLOPS

Serves 4

The bright acidity and nuttiness of the nibs is the perfect complement to a sweet scallop.
Look for fresh sea scallops in the late summer and early fall.

Scallops	12 large
Sea salt	2 teaspoons
Black pepper	2 teaspoons
Cocoa powder	1½ teaspoons
Unsalted butter	2 tablespoons
Cacao nibs	¼ cup
Lemon juice	From ½ lemon

1. Remove adductor muscle from each scallop if still intact.
2. Pat scallops dry with a paper towel.
3. Season scallops with salt, pepper, and cocoa powder.
4. Heat a cast-iron skillet over high heat.
5. Add butter to pan and let melt until brown around the edges.
6. Sear scallops on each side until golden brown and crisp.
7. Remove scallops from heat and garnish with cacao nibs.
8. Squeeze lemon onto brown butter in the pan and stir.
9. Spoon sauce over scallops.

OUT TO SEA

A gale-force wind blowing against the Gulf Stream is a very notorious thing. It's sunk ships, there's legends about it," Captain Eric tells us. It was three days into the maiden voyage and we were 300 miles off the East Coast of the United States in the Atlantic Ocean and racing a storm, a gale force 9 to be exact. There had been plenty of difficulties in getting this historic sailing trip underway to pick up twenty metric tons of cacao, and these were not the most comforting words to hear from our captain while at sea.

Twelve hours before our scheduled departure, Captain Eric Loftfield was wondering what he had gotten himself into. He had been building the *Black Seal,* a three-masted, seventy-foot steel cargo schooner, for the past twenty-five years in his own backyard. The *Black Seal* was like Eric's fifth child, it was a part of the family, and its moment was finally about to come. However, it wasn't going to be easy. There was still woodwork, plumbing, and electrical work to be finished while underway. The sinks and toilets weren't functioning just yet, there would be no autopilot installed, and the Captain's quarters were filled with boxes and grease-covered tools, leaving little room for him to maneuver, let alone sleep properly. In those hours prior to departure, Captain Eric, with his messy hair, cracked lips, and tired eyes, said to us, "You're never going to be as ready as you want to be, but if you don't go, you're never going to get off the dock. So, it's time."

The *Black Seal* got off the dock at high tide the following morning. Our route and navigational charts were set and with the captain's hands on the helm and his ear attuned to the radio's static bursts of weather patterns, winds, and updates, we began our journey 180 degrees due south from Cape Cod, Massachusetts, to Puerto Plata, a commercial loading dock on the northern coast of the Dominican Republic.

We were under way and the winds were pushing us off to a good start. We continued to organize the loose equipment and tools, spliced knots to tie up our cots so that we could sleep, and fussed with the stove that had just been installed and that relied on a pattern of specific motions to light properly in order not to smoke out the galley. Those first hours brought the realization that our dream of using wind to sail our beans and Captain Eric's dream of sailing cargo in the ship that he built were both coming to fruition. The sails were raised and we were losing sight of land. There was no turning back.

Over the next forty-eight hours the winds picked up and the consequences of our disorganized departure started surfacing. Books were spilling onto the chart table, pots shifting side to side on the stove were spitting up hot water, and loose items in the drawers were banging away with an endless and terrible rhythm. Everything needed to be tied down, including additional rope on the pipe bursts to keep our bodies from launching off our cots while we were trying to sleep. We would continue to rock in constant motion for the next fourteen days. The captain and crew weren't saying that the conditions were harsh, but things certainly didn't feel normal. I felt a newfound appreciation for the stability of land.

The crew split shifts at the helm—four hours on, eight hours off. To relieve them, I finally got a chance to steer the taped and weathered captain's wheel. The crew in the galley behind me looked nervous and took a seat. My anxiety was high—I would have preferred to learn in calmer conditions. We were cruising and my heart was racing. "It's like driving an old car that skids;

you want to meet the skids," Curtis, first mate and captain's brother, instructed. I thought I knew what he meant, but my focus was overwhelmed by the power of the ocean's waves. The bow of the ship began to veer off, with more than fifteen degrees of rudder than we needed, and the *Black Seal* rocked sharply to the left, throwing my grip from the wheel and me into the portside door. Thank God it was closed. Curtis quickly stepped in and, with a few seasoned maneuvers, got us back on track. I thought for sure I had sent somebody overboard. Luckily, I hadn't. I caught my breath just long enough to be told to get back on the wheel. This was going to be a long trip.

We started paying closer attention to the radio and learned it wasn't going to get any better for another forty-eight hours. The pilot charts described the likelihood of gales in this part of the ocean during the time of year we were sailing. The odds of coming into a storm like this were 1 percent. And yet the worst was yet to hit us. The rain, pouring in sheets, was filling the ocean and pounding the deck. The sun was setting and waves rose like mountains piling up overhead before sharply dipping into valleys of the ocean. We no longer had the luxury of light. The sky was wiped of its magnificent stars. Thunder and lightning clashed overhead. The mizzen sail jibed back and forth over the cabin and galley, startling us with malicious banging and clanging. Visibility was ten feet at best, but this may have been a blessing. We couldn't see the horizon line tilting vertically.

Flashlights were dangerously blinding, and without the reflection of the moon, we relied on a blood-red light in the galley to see, adding more tension. Curtis was at the wheel, spinning it from side to side, his 230-pound frame being thrown along with it as he cursed the ocean. Our ship was a tiny speck in the vast Atlantic. The top of the mainsail was being ripped to tatters as it became unlaced from the gaff and was whipping and cracking, beating itself to death. The same was happening to the square sail. In order not to lose it, too, we had to get the square sail down. Captain Eric stepped out onto the flooded deck, clung tightly to the rigging, and climbed the narrow ladder eighty feet to the top of the mast and up on the yard. His little ship was rocking at the mercy of the storm, the boom slamming and bruising his shins. The trajectory of the mast at the height was too fast, like an out-of-control metronome, flailing from side to side. We were stuck in the wheelhouse, unable to see the captain, and it crossed our minds that he may not be able to hold on. We didn't dare say that out loud.

Megan, the cook and my fiancée, was tied to her cot in the cargo hold, tears streaming as she wrote in her journal, praying we would make it out alive. Angry waves crashed up over the wooden rails and against us. I asked Curtis if I should go out to help, thinking only to secure the captain's arm or leg so he would not be thrown overboard. "Yeah, Michael, go on out there," Curtis instructed. Being subordinate, naively courageous, and not picking up on his sarcasm, I headed for the cabin's starboard door. "Don't fucking move! This isn't amateur hour!" Tensions were high. His brother's ship and life were both at stake. Another forty minutes passed. Nobody said a word. An intense focus filled the room as Curtis wrestled the wheel and waves, straining to see the perpetual incoming blows. Then, like a superhero who passes by in a flash, Eric flew past the windows in head-to-toe orange rain gear before hurling himself up on top of the wheelhouse. The mizzen sail started to become unfurled. The storm battered us for another twenty-four hours before subsiding.

The next week was as peaceful and inspiring as the first had been full of drama. The sun rose and set, painting the sky with the palette of a Monet, with only blessedly horizontal horizon lines in sight. Constellations lit up the night sky, schools of porpoises swam and jumped alongside us at the bow of the ship, and the occasional tern paused to rest its tired wings, hitching a ride as we approached the northern coast of the Dominican Republic. We had weathered the storm, and the first leg of the voyage was nearly complete. Now the hard part: loading the beans on board by hand and getting them back to Brooklyn. —*MM*

DARK & STORMY CHOCOLATE CAKE

Serves 10

The classic cocktail of dark rum and ginger beer is the choice of sailors and
the inspiration behind this cake. Top with chocolate frosting (see page 111).

Sugar	½ cup
Molasses	½ cup
Vegetable oil	½ cup
All-purpose flour	1¼ cups
Fresh ginger	4½ teaspoons peeled and grated
Ground cinnamon	1 teaspoon
Ground cloves	½ teaspoon
Black pepper	¼ teaspoon
Water	½ cup
Dark rum	¼ cup
Eggs	2
Lime zest	2 teaspoons
Baking soda	1 teaspoon
Dark chocolate	4 ounces, chopped

1. Preheat oven to 350 degrees Fahrenheit. Butter a 9-inch round cake pan.
2. Mix sugar, molasses, and vegetable oil in a large bowl.
3. In a separate bowl, combine flour, ginger, cinnamon, cloves, and pepper.
4. Combine both mixtures in a food processor.
5. Add water, rum, eggs, lime zest, and baking soda.
6. Fold in chocolate.
7. Pour batter into cake pan.
8. Bake for 30 minutes.

CHOCOLATE RUM CAKE

Serves 10

//

CAKE

Raisins	1 cup
Dark rum	1 cup
Unsalted butter	6 tablespoons (¾ stick), room temperature
Sugar	1 cup
Lemon zest	2 teaspoons
Ground cinnamon	2 teaspoons
Eggs	4
Cake flour	2 cups
Cocoa powder	½ cup
Baking powder	2 teaspoons
Sea salt	1 teaspoon
Sour cream	½ cup

RUM GLAZE

Unsalted butter	½ cup (1 stick)
Confectioners' sugar	4 cups
Water	¼ cup
White rum	¼ cup

//

Make the Cake

1. Soak raisins in rum for 1 hour.
2. Preheat oven to 375 degrees Fahrenheit. Butter a 9-inch round cake pan or a standard Bundt.
3. Beat butter, sugar, lemon zest, and cinnamon until fluffy.
4. Add eggs and combine.
5. Add flour, cocoa powder, baking powder, and salt, and combine.
6. Fold in sour cream.
7. Drain any remaining rum and fold in raisins.
8. Pour batter into cake pan.
9. Bake for 30 minutes. Let cool.

Make the Rum Glaze

10. Melt butter over medium heat.
11. In bowl, combine melted butter, sugar, water, and rum.

Assemble

12. When cake is cool, pour rum glaze over cake.

CHOCOLATE CARAMELS WITH SEA SALT

Makes 24

A staple in our Brooklyn kitchen.
We can't make enough of these to satisfy our customers.

/ /

Heavy cream	1¼ cups
Unsalted butter	2 cups (4 sticks)
Sugar	2 cups
Dark chocolate	5 ounces, chopped
Sea salt	1 teaspoon

/ /

1. Butter an 8-inch square pan. In a saucepan, heat cream with butter until melted.
2. In a separate pan over medium heat, melt sugar to 300 degrees Fahrenheit.
Test with an instant-read thermometer.
3. Slowly add cream-butter mixture to the caramelized sugar.
4. Bring the mixture to 260 degrees Fahrenheit.
5. Add chocolate and stir to emulsify.
6. Pour mixture into the pan and sprinkle salt on top.
7. Let cool. Cut into squares.

FRUIT & NUT BARK

Serves 12

Don't be bound by the ingredients below; put anything and everything in your bark.
Keep the parchment in place by tacking it with melted chocolate on the corners.

Almonds	½ cup
Pecans	½ cup
Hazelnuts	½ cup
Pistachios	½ cup
Dried cranberries	½ cup
Cacao nibs	½ cup
Sea salt	2 teaspoons
Dark chocolate	1 pound, melted and tempered (see page 9)

1. Preheat oven to 350 degrees Fahrenheit. Line a baking sheet with parchment paper.
2. Place almonds, pecans, and hazelnuts on a baking sheet and roast to golden brown, about 10 minutes.
3. Combine with pistachios and roughly chop all nuts.
4. Put in a bowl with dried cranberries, cacao nibs, and sea salt.
5. Add tempered chocolate and combine.
6. Spread to ½ inch thick on baking sheet.
7. Let set in refrigerator.
8. Lift bark off parchment and break into pieces.

CHOCOLATE CHIP & RICOTTA PANCAKES

Makes 12

Pancakes in the morning were part of the daily routine aboard our historic sail.
This recipe makes incredibly delicious and fluffy pancakes.
Dress with your favorite maple syrup or local honey.

Eggs	3, separated
Ricotta cheese	1 cup
Whole milk	¼ cup
Sugar	3 tablespoons
Sea salt	1 pinch
All-purpose flour	⅔ cup
Dark chocolate	2½ ounces, finely chopped
Unsalted butter	6 tablespoons (¾ stick)

1. In a medium bowl, whisk egg yolks with ricotta cheese, milk, sugar, and salt.
2. Add flour and chocolate and combine.
3. In a separate bowl using a handheld mixer, beat egg whites to soft peaks.
4. Fold egg whites into flour-ricotta mixture.
5. Melt 1 tablespoon of butter for each batch in a large pan over medium heat.
6. Ladle batter onto pan in 6-inch circles.
7. When edges brown and batter bubbles, flip pancakes.
8. Pancakes are ready once both sides are golden brown.

THE BROOKLYN WATERFRONT

As a card-carrying, hyper-nostalgic Midwestern immigrant, with a past speckled in recreational hallucinogenics, I like to imagine Walt Whitman and Tom Sawyer strolling along the Brooklyn banks of the East River, waving to the sailors from shore. Tom is of course barefoot, kicking rocks into the water while fishing, and Walt is happily writing poetry and teaching Tom how to pack his first corncob pipe.

In the year 1939, Franklin Roosevelt was president, Hitler's forces prepared to invade Poland, Billie Holiday released the album *Strange Fruit,* John Steinbeck's *The Grapes of Wrath* was published, and Batman made his first appearance in a comic book. The year also marked the last time commercially sailed cargo passed the Statue of Liberty for port.

Brooklyn has really changed.

We have all said, often sarcastically, that continuous change is really the one and only constant in New York City. Change is perhaps most obvious at the waterfront, as modern apartment complexes rise, old factories rezone to luxury lofts, and beautiful stretches of new park replace the abandoned, industrial ports that once lined the East River. Decades earlier, those industrial ports had once replaced the old wooden wharves that lined the water's edge by the hundreds, serving that many and more sailing cargo vessels, making New York's waterways as busy as Times Square.

The view from the Brooklyn waterfront must have been quite a sight at the turn of the century. A hundred or more large schooners, sails wrestling with the wind, the Brooklyn Bridge and a young but rising Manhattan skyline as a backdrop. Compared to today's diesel engines and wailing sirens, there must have been an odd silence about it. So much movement and activity, but the primary sounds would be the fluttering of sails and the voices of deckhands echoing over the water onto the banks.

After all of the obstacles (storms, customs, doubters), the *Black Seal,* a seventy-foot three-masted schooner, was set to arrive at the Red Hook Terminal in Brooklyn. Large container ships passed by, carrying nearly a thousand containers each. Our little boat was the largest ship in the Cape Cod marina from which it set sail over a month ago, but it was dwarfed by the massive industrial shipping machine next to it, which carried Red Bull, Heineken, and bananas in bulk. Massive cranes that resembled something from *Star Wars* moved containers on and off ships like a child playing with blocks. Certainly an incredible engineering feat, yet even this monumental operation seemed antiquated somehow, dying. I later found out that the Brooklyn container yard's customs post may shut down. Nearly all commercial cargo is brought into New Jersey or Pennsylvania these days. A touching irony that one of Brooklyn's final shipments into the historic Red Hook docks would perhaps be by sail after all these years.

Just off the coast of Coney Island (we were within view from the top of the Cyclone), the *Black Seal* had been held up by customs agencies and the Coast Guard, all wondering what the hell we were doing. But finally

we had made it through and were docked in Brooklyn. Suits, longshoreman, city workers, union reps, customs officials, stevedores, chocolate makers, bloggers, and a writer from the *Wall Street Journal* welcomed the historic sail. However, before anyone could bust out the Champagne, we had to get our cacao off the boat.

Nearly three hundred 150-pound bags of cocoa beans filled the cargo hold of the *Black Seal*. Due to the laws of gravity, it would prove to be far easier to put the bags into the ship than to take them out. It was apparent almost immediately that we would need some help, mechanized help. Not only did we not have gravity on our side but the height of the pier made it obvious that it was built for much larger ships. There was a seven-foot difference between the deck of the boat and the concrete dock. We needed a small crane that could masterfully maneuver around the sail riggings, dip its hook into a four-by-four-foot entry to the cargo hold, and allow our crew to attach a net full of cacao on the end. We didn't have a crane.

After making some desperate phone calls we found a crane and an operator, but they were not in Red Hook. Bringing traffic to a complete halt, our equipment cruised west at about five miles per hour on the Brooklyn-Queens Expressway from Greenpoint. That crane operator saved the day, effortlessly maneuvering the arm and hook around sail riggings and a bobbing boat while chewing gum and talking to her friends back in Long Island on her Bluetooth earpiece. It was impressive, to say the least.

The final bag was unloaded and exhausted hoorays echoed against the pier. The entire voyage had required only thirty gallons of fuel, the amount needed to take a large container ship 900 feet.

The Brooklyn waterfront is ever changing. Four hundred years ago, it was dotted with Iroquois wigwams and tepees; then came country estates for wealthy New Yorkers. The waterfront has provided a staging ground for the building of ships and weaponry, hosted industrial giants like Domino Sugar, and been abandoned. Now parks are being created from the Brooklyn Bridge to the Williamsburg Bridge. Sailing vessels are seen once again on the East River. Informed by the past, Brooklyn looks to the future. —*RM*

BLACK & WHITE COOKIES

Makes 24

As famous as the Brooklyn Bridge, this New York City icon is also referred to
as a half-moon, a half-and-half, or a drop cake. More cakes than cookies,
they are light and moist thanks to a hint of lemon.

COOKIES

Unsalted butter	½ cup (1 stick), room temperature
Granulated sugar	1 cup
Grated lemon zest	1½ teaspoons
Lemon juice	1 teaspoon
Eggs	4
All-purpose flour	2 cups
Baking powder	2 teaspoons
Sea salt	½ teaspoon
Whole milk	¾ cup

WHITE ICING

Confectioners' sugar	1 cup
Water	2 tablespoons
Lemon juce	1 teaspoon

CHOCOLATE ICING

Whole milk	1 cup
Cocoa powder	1 teaspoon
Dark chocolate	8 ounces, chopped
Unsalted butter	2 tablespoons
Vanilla	1 teaspoon

Make the Cookies

1. Preheat oven to 350 degrees Fahrenheit.
2. In a medium bowl, cream butter with sugar.
3. Add lemon zest and lemon juice.
4. Add eggs one at a time.
5. Mix in flour, baking powder, and salt.
6. Add milk and mix lightly until the batter is smooth.
7. Spoon batter 2 inches apart on a parchment-lined baking tray.
8. Bake for 12 minutes. Let cool.

Make the White Icing
9. Mix confectioners' sugar with water and lemon juice.
10. Spread white icing on half of each cookie.

Make the Chocolate Icing
11. Bring milk to a boil with cocoa powder. Pour over chopped chocolate.
12. Add butter and vanilla and mix until mixture is smooth.
13. Spread the chocolate icing on the other half of each cookie.

YELLOW CAKE WITH CHOCOLATE FROSTING

Serves 10

///////////////////////////////////////

CAKE

Unsalted butter	¾ cup (1½ sticks), room temperature
Granulated sugar	1¾ cups
Egg yolks	6
Cake flour	2 cups
Baking powder	3½ teaspoons
Sea salt	½ teaspoon
Whole milk	¾ cup

FROSTING

Dark chocolate	8 ounces, chopped
Unsalted butter	½ cup (1 stick), room temperature
Vanilla	1 tablespoon
Confectioners' sugar	2 cups
Cream cheese	1 pound

//////////////////////////////////////

Make the Cake

1. Preheat oven to 350 degrees Fahrenheit. Butter an 8-inch round cake pan.
2. In the bowl of a standing mixer, beat butter with granulated sugar until fluffy.
3. Add egg yolks and flour, baking powder, and salt and combine.
4. Add milk and combine.
5. Pour batter into cake pan.
6. Bake for 25 minutes. Let cool.

Make the Frosting

7. Melt the chocolate in a double boiler.
8. In a bowl, cream butter with vanilla and confectioners' sugar.
9. Add cream cheese and melted chocolate and combine until smooth.

Assemble

10. Cut cake horizontally into 3 layers.
11. Spread frosting in between layers, on top, and around sides.

CHOCOLATE CRUNCH

Serves 24

Perfect for a long hike, breakfast on the run, or mid-afternoon cravings.
Make plenty ahead of time and keep them handy.

Dark chocolate	1½ pounds, chopped
Unsalted butter	½ cup (1 stick)
Peanut butter	2 tablespoons
Honey	1 tablespoon
Puffed rice cereal	4 cups

1. In a double boiler, melt chocolate and butter.
2. Add peanut butter and honey. Mix until combined.
3. Mix in puffed rice and pour into 9-inch square baking pan.
4. Let set in refrigerator.

CHOCOLATE BREAD

Makes 1 medium loaf

A perfect anytime-of-day bread recipe.

//

Fresh yeast	1 tablespoon plus ¾ teaspoon
Brown sugar	⅔ cup
Water	1½ cups, lukewarm
All-purpose flour	4 cups
Cocoa powder	1 tablespoon
Sea salt	1 pinch
Egg yolks	3
Unsalted butter	2 tablespoons, room temperature
Dark chocolate	12 ounces, chopped
Hazelnuts	½ cup
Raisins	½ cup
Whole milk	½ cup

//

1. Preheat oven to 425 degrees Fahrenheit.
2. Mix yeast and brown sugar with water.
3. Let sit for 10 minutes, until bubbling.
4. Add flour, cocoa powder, and salt.
5. In a separate bowl, combine 1 egg yolk with butter and add to dough.
6. In the bowl of a standing mixer using the dough paddle, knead dough for 10 minutes. Let stand for 10 minutes and then repeat kneading for an additional 10 minutes.
7. Add dark chocolate, hazelnuts, and raisins.
8. Let dough rise, covered, on your counter for 2 hours.
9. Turn dough out onto lightly floured table and punch one time.
10. Place dough in a 9-inch loaf pan.
11. Combine remaining 2 egg yolks and milk and brush egg wash onto the shaped dough.
12. Leave dough to proof on a baking sheet for 45 minutes, until it has doubled in size.
13. Bake for 12 minutes.
14. Lower temperature to 350 degrees Fahrenheit and bake for an additional 20 minutes.

STUMPTOWN MOCHA TRUFFLES

Makes 24

We've been working with the roasters of Stumptown Coffee for years and we've come
up with a truffle celebrating this incredible relationship and their incredible craft.

///

GANACHE

Half-and-half	1 cup
Dark chocolate with Stumptown Coffee	6 ounces, chopped
Unsalted butter	1 tablespoon

COATING

Dark chocolate	8 ounces, melted and tempered (see page 9)
Coffee beans	1 tablespoon, ground
Cacao nibs	½ cup, roughly chopped

///

Make the Ganache

1. Bring half-and-half to a boil in a saucepan over medium-high heat.
2. Pour cream over chocolate in a heatproof bowl.
3. Let it sit and melt for 1 minute.
4. Using a spatula, stir tight circles from the center outward.
5. Let mixture cool to 108 degrees Fahrenheit. Check with an instant-read thermometer.
6. Add butter and stir until combined.
7. Shape ganache into marble-size spheres by rolling between your hands.

Coat the Truffles

8. Dip ganache in tempered chocolate.
9. Roll in ground coffee beans and cacao nibs. Let cool until coating is set.

– Part Four –

MASTERING OUR CRAFT

A FACTORY GROWS IN BROOKLYN

/ / / / / / /

*C*hocolate was no longer to be a hobby for us. Rick and I decided to take July and August away from each other, shook hands, and vowed to officially quit our jobs and start a company in September. As fall approached, so did the nerve-racking prospect of having no income. Our first meetings began just ten feet from our respective bedrooms, at our weathered butcher-block dining room table. It was 9 a.m. and we both showed up on time. So far, so good. *How to Start a Chocolate Company*, I wrote on a yellow legal pad so that it was official. We wanted to continue to make a different kind of chocolate, craft chocolate. There was no *chocolate kit* to speak of for building a chocolate company with our techniques and size. Few were actually making chocolate from scratch and so there was no standard equipment to use or business model to emulate.

Step 1: Find cacao beans, Rick wrote. Perfect, we were off to a great start. We had been playing around with ten pounds here and there, but we knew that wasn't going to cut it if we were going to get serious. We took to the Internet, researching and devouring as much as we could about different regions, farming methods and practices, and bean varietals. The large majority, well over 70 percent of cocoa beans, are of the Forastero varietal. Forastero are heartier, can withstand extreme climate conditions, and are more productive; however, they are less flavorful than their counterpart, the Criollo. Criollo beans, which make up less than 5 percent of cacao production, are much more difficult to grow, but whether eaten raw, straight out of the pod, or after being turned into chocolate, they offer much more delicious and vibrant notes. Then there is the Trinitario, the hybrid of the two that sits pleasantly in the middle of the spectrum between the Criollo and the Forastero.

We quickly fell in love with the Criollo and Trini-

tario varietals and purchased our first seventy-kilogram bag of cacao (approximately 150 pounds). It arrived the next week, stirring both enthusiasm and cynicism. The delivery driver was from Grenada and couldn't believe that he was bringing a bag of cacao to a small apartment in Williamsburg. He had only seen cacao in his home country and wished us the best of luck as we passionately told him about our plans to build a chocolate factory—no doubt offering more information than he was looking for. We carried the bag up the three flights of stairs and propped it in our living room. Our roommate came out of his room to see the commotion. "What the hell is that?" he asked with raised eyebrows, before backtracking to his room to finish a battle in Medal of Honor on PlayStation.

Step 2: Rent a space. This seemed like an easy one, as there were abandoned spaces everywhere in Williamsburg, holdovers from its industrial roots. There was only one problem. We didn't have much money. We needed to move our operation out of our apartment for several reasons. We had already taken over the entire apartment, and then every evening at seven o'clock we would clean up and attempt to move the operation to our rooms before our roommate came home. Our girlfriends began to crash at our apartment, making headquarters pretty tight for the six of us. But more important, it was illegal. So, we started looking at warehouses and lofts in the neighborhood. We found a space on the second floor of a commercial loft space on Morgan Avenue. It was an industrial area filled with stone importers and marble cutters on every block. The building itself was home to metalworkers and woodworkers, restaurant storage, painters, screen printers, and other craftsmen. Not much of a factory, but it would work for now. Our space was small, only 300 square feet, but it had hardwood

floors and tall ceilings. We were excited to be out of the apartment and in a commercial space. After signing the eighteen-month lease we headed to John's Deli around the corner, grabbed a couple of 40s, and celebrated in our new factory. Out of the one large window in the narrow alley was a silver DeLorean like the one featured in *Back to the Future,* one of my favorite movies. We used every excuse for another round of cheers. We felt in control of our own future.

Step 3: Make chocolate. Having left behind our apartment oven, we were roasting in a coffee drum roaster, which held only three pounds of beans at a time. We cracked the cacao shells with a hand mill used for crushing barley in home brewing. We winnowed the husks from the nibs using fans, or even hair dryers, to blow away the lighter husks. At times we used juicers to break down the nibs into a chocolaty paste before adding sugar and grinding for days in twenty- and forty-pound wet grinders. The grinders weren't even made for chocolate. The chocolate was too thick and the belts smoked, burned, and snapped. We added variable-frequency devices to control the speed and heat, but the motors needed upgrading and replacing. We still had a long way to go in order to master our craft. There were inconsistencies, but that was also part of the excitement of small batches—it allowed us to understand the nuances at different stages in the process. Again, there was no chocolate kit or model to replicate. Our chocolate was made differently from every other chocolate. It tasted different. It used only two ingredients. It tasted better, but our problems with home appliances continued, and we needed money to make the proper customizations and upgrades.

Looking for loans, we headed to the business libraries and scheduled meetings with Small Business Association specialists in Manhattan. That same week, the fallout from the subprime mortgage loans surfaced, and the country was in a financial crisis. "Not good," I said. Maybe the worst recession to hit since the Great Depression, experts were predicting. I was predicting rejection letters from our applications. I was right. We couldn't even get a $25,000 loan. Rick and I were already stuck, unable to move forward. Without many options, we applied for five separate credit cards, seduced by a 0 percent APR for the first six months, slightly reducing the stress.

We maxed out our cards quickly buying a refrigerator, molds, and a miniature winnower. The next piece we needed was an oven. The three-pound coffee drum roaster wasn't moving us forward, and the husks had a tendency to crack from the churning, resulting in burnt batches. Rick's instinct was to use a convection oven as many restaurant kitchens do. We turned to Craigslist. New, these ovens were about four grand or more, but to our surprise we found a used one for sale for a thousand bucks. We called and headed to the location on Broadway to pick up the old beast, which was missing a few lights and buttons. It was in an empty space with cracked tile floors, but we were assured that it worked, with the only disclaimer being that it had roasted hundreds of chickens. We took the seller's word for it, told him we were going to clean it like new, and then asked about the space we were in. It was to be a butcher shop, Marlow & Daughters. Music to our ears. We had just started selling our bars at Marlow & Sons just down the street. They said to forget about the money for this old oven and instead we bartered, dropping off boxes and boxes of chocolate in exchange. If only it were always going to be so easy. Our factory filled up with the pallets of burlap cacao sacks, equipment, inventory, worktables, and a desk. We already needed more space. —*MM*

CHOCOLATE BUTTERCREAM

Makes 2½ cups

An essential frosting that's perfect for cakes, fillings, and decoration.

/ /

Unsalted butter	¼ cup (½ stick), room temperature
Cocoa powder	¼ cup
Confectioners' sugar	2 cups
Vanilla	1 teaspoon
Whole milk	¼ cup, warm

/ /

1. In a medium bowl, cream the butter.
2. Add cocoa powder and combine.
3. Add confectioners' sugar and vanilla and combine.
4. Add milk in a slow, steady stream while stirring briskly to a smooth consistency.

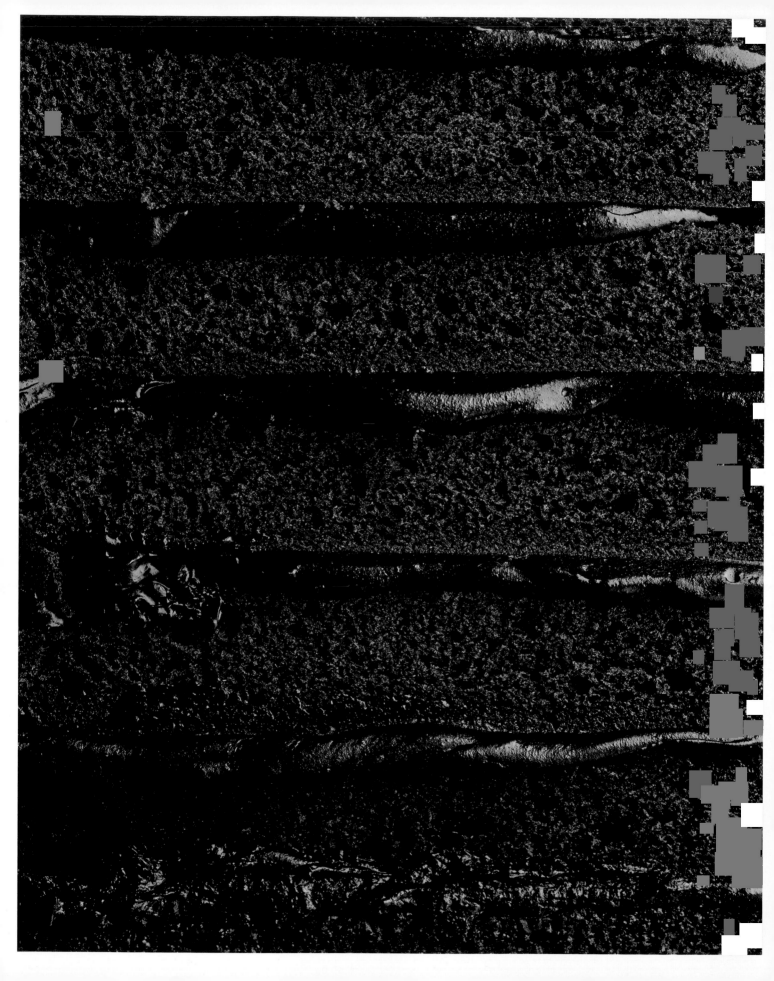

CHOCOLATE LAYER CAKE

Serves 10

///

CAKE

Eggs	6
Sugar	2 cups
Cake flour	2 cups
Cocoa powder	¾ cup
Baking powder	2 teaspoons

FROSTING

Sugar	2 cups
Heavy cream	2 cups
Dark chocolate	3 ounces, chopped

///

Make the Cake

1. Preheat oven to 400 degrees Fahrenheit. Butter a 12-inch round cake pan.
2. In a large bowl or the bowl of a standing mixer, beat eggs and sugar until thick.
3. Combine flour, cocoa powder, and baking powder in a medium bowl and sift them into egg mixture.
4. Fold them in lightly until mixture is smooth.
5. Pour batter into cake pan.
6. Bake for 30 minutes.
7. Let cake cool completely.
8. Slice cake horizontally into 4 even layers.

Make the Frosting

9. Caramelize sugar in a saucepan over medium heat until golden brown.
10. In a separate saucepan, heat heavy cream. Carefully pour over caramelized sugar.
11. Bring to a boil and dissolve all of the sugar into the cream.
12. Pass caramel sauce through a sieve into a bowl containing the chocolate.
13. Let melt for 1 minute.
14. Stir in tight circles until emulsified.

Assemble

15. Spread frosting between each cake layer and on top and sides of cake.

TOASTED ALMOND TRUFFLES

Makes 24

Perfectly toasted almonds pair incredibly well with chocolate.
Add a touch of sea salt to bring out the robust flavors.

///////////////////////////////////////

GANACHE

Heavy cream	½ cup
Dark chocolate	6 ounces, chopped
Unsalted butter	½ tablespoon

COATING

Dark chocolate	8 ounces, melted and tempered (see page 9)
Almonds	1 cup, toasted and chopped

///////////////////////////////////////

Make the Ganache

1. Bring cream to a boil in a saucepan.
2. Pour cream over chocolate in a heatproof bowl.
3. Let sit and melt for 1 minute.
4. Stir with a spatula in tight circles from the center outward.
5. Let mixture cool to 108 degrees Fahrenheit. Test with an instant-read thermometer.
6. Add butter and stir until combined.
7. Shape ganache into marble-size spheres by rolling between your hands.

Coat the Truffles

8. Dip ganache in tempered chocolate.
9. Roll spheres in chopped almonds. Let cool until coating is set.

CHOCOLATE OATMEAL COOKIES

Makes 24

We grew up on these. Prior to baking, sprinkle the cookies
with a few more oats for a beautiful garnish.

Unsalted butter	1 cup (2 sticks), room temperature
Brown sugar	2 cups
Eggs	2
All-purpose flour	2 cups
Cocoa powder	6 tablespoons
Baking powder	2 teaspoons
Baking soda	1 teaspoon
Sea salt	1 teaspoon
Dark chocolate	15 ounces, chopped
Rolled oats	2½ cups

1. Preheat oven to 350 degrees Fahrenheit.

2. In a medium bowl, cream butter with brown sugar.

3. Add eggs, flour, cocoa powder, baking powder and soda, and salt and combine.

4. Add chocolate and oats and combine.

5. Spoon cookie dough 2 inches apart on a baking sheet using heaping tablespoons.

6. Bake for 12 minutes.

CHOCOLATE LAVA CAKE

Serves 4

Legend has it that this cake was invented by mistake.
But make no mistake about its rich, hot molten middle, which gives this cake its name.
Once it's cooked, a light dusting of confectioners' sugar adds just the right touch.

Dark chocolate	6 ounces, chopped
Unsalted butter	½ cup (1 stick)
Eggs	2
Egg yolks	2
Granulated sugar	¼ cup
All-purpose flour	2 tablespoons
Sea salt	¼ teaspoon
Confectioners' sugar	To garnish

1. Preheat oven to 450 degrees Fahrenheit. Butter and flour individual ramekins.
2. Melt chocolate and butter in a double boiler.
3. In a bowl, mix eggs, egg yolks, and sugar until thick.
4. Combine egg and chocolate mixtures and add flour and salt.
5. Mix until a smooth batter forms.
6. Pour batter into ramekins.
7. Bake for 12 minutes.
8. Let sit for 15 seconds before removing from ramekins.

MAKING CRAFT CHOCOLATE

*O*ur day starts early. Just before 7 a.m. my brother and I arrive at the factory, open the door, and turn on the lights. Hot coffee in hand, I head to the locker room. I don a chef's jacket and tie an apron snug around my waist. I put on an old wool bicycle hat that I've worn every day for three years and make my way through the labyrinth of the building to the factory and a large butcher-block table. The wood is a rich auburn color from cocoa butter and mineral oil. It is also carved up from chopping untempered blocks of chocolate for the melter.

I turn the convection oven on for preheating and hoist a large bag of single-estate cacao from La Red de Guaconejo in the Dominican Republic. These beans had been aboard the *Black Seal,* making their way by wind and sail over the course of fourteen days to the docks in Red Hook, Brooklyn.

Throwing the sack down on the butcher-block table, I use a twelve-inch chef's knife to slice open the top. Beans pour out onto the table and the room fills with the aroma of fermented cacao—balsamic vinegar, cinnamon, sour cherry, and earth. I dip my hands into the flow of beans to inspect the harvest. The fruit notes are bright, fresh, clear.

Bean by bean, I begin inspection of the entire bag for quality. Too flat, too small, over-fermented, bark—I toss them into an empty bowl and hear the clank as my focus turns back to the beans in front of me. This bag is clean, nearly perfect. After an hour of sorting, I look at the bowl of throwaways and see only a dozen or so mutated beans and pieces of bark.

The oven is ready. It has been scrubbed outrageously clean so as to not affect the flavor potential of this particular chocolate and preheated perfectly to 300 degrees Fahrenheit, which I check and double check with my thermometer. I have spread the cacao evenly, one bean high, over perforated sheet trays. The trays go into the oven.

Towel in hand, I clean the handle of the oven as I shut the door and take another sip of coffee. It is a cold, late-autumn morning and I rode my bike to work from Clinton Hill. My hands and cheeks are not yet warmed up, and I can feel the heat of the coffee go down my throat through my chest, warming me up from the inside out. The warmth from the convection oven begins to fill the room as well. Content and optimistic, I put on a compilation of Neil Young, Leo Kottke, Steve Martin's bluegrass stuff, and Will Oldham, interspersed with hymns and traditionals.

The oven timer goes off and I open the door to check the roasting progress. I take each tray out and turn it, mixing up the beans by hand for even roasting, and carefully place the trays back in the oven. I close the door, set the timer, and draw a deep inhale through my nose, smelling the first roast of the day as the room slowly fills with aromas reminiscent of Grandma's brownies.

The second timer goes off. This time the door opens with a swoosh of steam and the entire factory (often the entire neighborhood) becomes a chocolate tornado. As if I just heard a dirty joke for the first time, I instantly become giddy with laughter. Oven mitts on, I take the trays out to cool on a rack next to a wall covered in subway tile; a fan breezes over the beans so they don't over-roast.

During the small batches of roasting I continue sorting through the seventy-five-kilo bag of cacao, prepping sheet trays one bean high, sipping coffee, and watching through the front door as North 3rd Street wakes up and goes to work.

Once the beans become cool enough to touch, I take a handful and crush them in my palms, inhaling to check for roasting quality. The dry shells separate in my palm from the still-warm nibs and release aromas that are filled with citrus complexity with little to no roastiness. Heighten, clarify, and preserve is what the roast should do, not disfigure.

Just as the Watersons begin wailing "The Old Churchyard," I take twenty pounds of cacao over to our winnowing machine. This wondrous device is a testament to the do-it-yourself mentality of modern Brooklyn. From a woodworking shop, it looks like a cross between a high-school science fair entry and a bong that would make Tommy Chong sweat. Our winnowing machine has seen many edits, tweaks, and spare parts, but it still gets the job done without compromise.

I scoop the beans into the small bean cracker at the top of the device, built by a sympathetic friend who had seen us hand-grinding each bean for hours on end. After the beans are cracked into shells and nibs, they are sucked into the first chamber of the winnower. Gravity takes hold of the heavier nibs and allows them to fall into the waiting bin, gathering and holding the essential ingredient as the lighter shells are sucked into the second chamber. I bring the container of clean, pure nibs into our stone-grinding room, leaving the shells to be bagged up later and picked up by the Brooklyn Botanic Gardens, where they use them for compost and mulch.

My brother has taken over roasting and I can tell in a glance that he is lost in the world of sorting, finding that Zen state of mind that comes with the morning roast. I smile and begin breaking down the cacao nibs by pouring them into a large mixing bowl containing two heavy granite rollers. These fermented and freshly roasted beans hit the stone quickly, preserving and locking in the unique character of the bean in its own fat and added sugars. As the stone rollers begin to break down the nibs, both grinding and melting them, I slowly add more, ounce by ounce. Too fast and the rollers will stick, too slow and some of the nibs will be more finely ground than others, creating an inconsistent mouthfeel.

The nibs melt before my eyes due to their 54 percent fat content. After an hour and a half of slowly pouring nibs, I am gratified to see something that looks almost like chocolate! The acidic volatiles release into the air, creating a chocolate intensity in the room.

Organic cane sugar is next. This is poured slowly as well, for even distribution and to facilitate emulsification. It is a slow and simple process, the kind of slow and simple that, once you submit to it, makes you yearn for it when the fast pace of New York life surrounds you. The two ingredients will remain under the stone for two more days, slowly becoming craft chocolate. I wipe down the outside of the mixing bowl, the axles, and the long stem holding it all together. I sweep the floor of any lost nibs and exit the grinding room to chat with my brother about lunch.

We settle on heading to Marlow & Daughters to pick up a spread of cured meats, olives, and cheeses. We wash it down with a beer, kindly provided by a couple of local breweries, that we keep on tap in the break room.

When we return to the factory floor, Michael has finished roasting the entire bag. A batch of chocolate (Dominican Republic) has been under the stone for just over two days. The color is rich with purple hues, and the aromas lifting off the surface are almost overwhelming. I dip a spoon in the churning bowl of chocolate to see if it is ready to come out. The particles from the sugar and cocoa solids are undetectable, a perfect emulsification. I allow the chocolate to coat my tongue and mouth, detecting the sweet acidity, notes of blackberry and molasses, and long, lingering red wine notes, as if a bottle of Californian Cabernet had been poured into the grinder at the last minute. It's ready.

Tilting the large mixing bowl and pouring the chocolate through a strainer, I transfer the chocolate to rectangular bins, which are then covered and labeled with the date and origin. I put the bin on one of our many aging racks to develop even more flavor over the next thirty days. The racks stretch to the ceiling and line the walls like a library. The chocolate on these racks isn't stable—it is alive, changing, separating, evolving. Soon it will be ready; soon it will be craft chocolate. —RM

CLASSIC CHOCOLATE TRUFFLES

Makes 12

Truffles should be rolled by hand and should look like their namesake mushroom.

//

Heavy cream	½ cup
Dark chocolate	8 ounces, chopped
Unsalted butter	2 tablespoons
Cocoa powder	½ cup

//

1. Bring cream to a boil in a saucepan.
2. Pour cream over chocolate in a heatproof bowl.
3. Let it sit and melt for 1 minute.
4. Stir with a spatula in tight circles from the center outward.
5. Let mixture cool to 108 degrees. Test with an instant-read thermometer.
6. Add butter and stir until combined.
7. Cover with plastic wrap and refrigerate for 1 hour.
8. Roll ganache by hand into small, truffle mushroom–shape balls.
9. Roll truffles in cocoa powder.

CHOCOLATE BUTTER GANACHE SQUARES

Makes 64

This confection will melt in your mouth and in your hand, so store in a cool place.

Heavy cream	1 cup
Dark chocolate	12½ ounces, chopped
Unsalted butter	1 tablespoon, cut into small cubes

1. Line an 8-inch square baking pan with parchment paper. Bring cream to a boil in a saucepan.
2. Pour cream over chocolate in a heatproof bowl.
3. Let it sit and melt for 1 minute.
4. Stir with a spatula in tight circles from the center outward.
5. Add butter cubes and stir until combined.
6. Pour the mixture into the baking pan.
7. Cover ganache with plastic wrap and flatten wrap to surface.
8. Let cool to room temperature until set.
9. Cut into 1-inch squares.

CHOCOLATE CREAM PIE

Serves 10

///

CRUST

All-purpose flour	2 cups
Cocoa powder	½ cup
Sugar	3 tablespoons
Unsalted butter	1 cup (2 sticks)
Egg yolks	2
Ice water	¼ cup

FILLING

Whole milk	2 cups
Egg yolks	2
Egg	1
Sugar	1 cup
Cornstarch	¼ cup
Cocoa powder	2 tablespoons
Unsalted butter	2 tablespoons
Dark chocolate	2 ounces, chopped

WHIPPED CREAM

Heavy cream	1½ cups
Sugar	3 tablespoons

///

Make the Crust

1. Preheat oven to 350 degrees Fahrenheit.

2. In a food processor, pulse flour, cocoa powder, sugar, and butter until flaky.

3. Add egg yolks and ice water and pulse just until mixture becomes dough.

4. Turn dough out onto work surface and knead by hand until smooth.

5. Wrap in plastic wrap and let rest in refrigerator for 30 minutes.

6. Roll out thinly to cover the bottom and sides of a 12-inch pie plate.

7. Bake for 20 minutes. Let cool.

Make the Filling

8. In a medium saucepan, bring the milk to a boil.

9. In a medium bowl using a whisk or handheld mixer, beat the egg yolks, egg, and half of the sugar until fluffy.

10. Add cornstarch, cocoa powder, and remaining sugar and combine.

11. Add to hot milk mixture and simmer until thick.

12. Stir in butter and chocolate and mix until smooth.

13. Take off heat and let cool.

Make the Whipped Cream

14. In the bowl of a standing mixer, whip cream to soft peaks and slowly blend in sugar.

Assemble

15. Spread filling onto cooled piecrust.

16. Top pie with whipped cream.

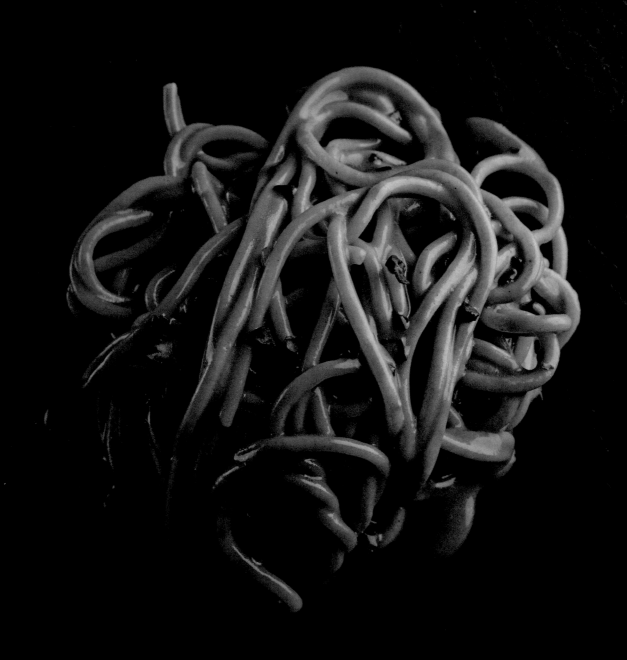

SAVORY CHOCOLATE CREAM SAUCE

Serves 12

Serve with your favorite pasta. Also pairs nicely with veal, chicken, or pork.

Unsalted butter	2 tablespoons
Yellow onions	2 medium, chopped
Sherry vinegar	3 tablespoons
Beef stock	4 cups
Heavy cream	2 cups
Dark chocolate	2 ounces, chopped
Cacao nibs	1 cup
Sea salt	1 tablespoon
Black pepper	2 teaspoons

1. Melt butter over medium heat and sauté onions for 5 minutes.
2. Add vinegar and reduce until thick.
3. Add beef stock and reduce by half.
4. Add cream and reduce until thickened, stirring constantly.
5. Whisk in chocolate and cacao nibs.
6. Add salt and pepper.

WRAP YOUR CHOCOLATE LIKE FOOD

I have an undying love affair with mom-and-pop shops. Whether it's the local butcher shop, bodega, cheesemonger, fish market, or bakery, I love to look through the display-cabinet glass, dream of what could be created with the ingredients on offer, and select my cut, portion, and variety with a show of false confidence. I love the unique look, smell, and sound of each shop. And I particularly love watching practiced hands behind the counter wrap culinary gifts. Large rolls of thick, sturdy, reddish brown paper are cut and expertly folded around the lamb shanks, striped bass, or Jasper Hill aged cheddar. I love being handed the beautiful package, the feel of the paper, and the giddy anticipation of opening it on my kitchen counter when I return home to my family.

It is this experience and memory that my brother and I sought to replicate with the wrapping of our chocolate bars, making a visit to your local chocolate maker as familiar and enticing an experience as a visit to your local butcher.

Our initial idea was to wrap our chocolate in butcher paper, placing a sticker simply stating the bean origin, the percentage of cacao, and the name of our company. The goal was to connect people to the idea that chocolate is food. To prove that it can be a beautiful and sophisticated American craft product, made from the seeds of fermented fruit, stone-ground and aged. Rather than *tell* people by crowding the chocolate bar wrappers with long-winded explanations, lofty certifications, and high-minded philosophy, why not *show* people in an elegant and subtle way? With beautiful paper texture and weight, crisp folds, and a sticker, we could turn the simple act of unwrapping a chocolate bar into a mission statement.

We wrapped our first hundred chocolate bars in plain butcher paper, but it was immediately apparent that something was missing. Our girlfriends (now our wives) thought that perhaps the papers were a bit too utilitarian, masculine, and rebellious. Of course, we couldn't have asked for higher praise, but we understood the criticism and turned it into an opportunity. Could we introduce beautiful colors, patterns, and illustrations to the paper, dressing it up and paying tribute to America's rich chocolate-manufacturing history while maintaining the feel of butcher paper?

We began the process of experimentation, always looking for ways to improve the wrapping. We made many trips to Manhattan's East Village, to the upstairs paper department at New York Central Art Supply shop. The staff there is amazingly knowledgeable and helpful; the service is not unlike the type you find at the very butcher shops we were seeking to emulate. They patiently allowed us to look at just about everything they had in stock: vintage Italian papers, dead-stock English wrapping paper, textured handmade Indian papers. Papers were being shipped from all around the world to their store, and they would set them aside for us to pick up in elaborately constructed cardboard carrying cases, complete with cutout handles and even an optional carrying strap made of packing tape. Their selection was outstanding, and we will always be thankful for the incredible hospitality they showed us there.

Our company's ethos and chocolate-making technique had become fiercely independent, and we finally determined that our chocolate bar wrappers had to live up to that same standard. We decided that we must do it ourselves, meaning design the papers in-house and have them printed by a reputable local printing press. We wanted our chocolate to be representative of the beautiful designers and factory workers in our own backyard. We got to work immediately, recruiting talented

family members such as Daniel Barragan, the brother of our sales manager, Arto. As unofficial company barber and tattoo artist, he helped orchestrate many of the first, original Mast Brothers wrappers. Michael's wife, Megan, has also designed many of the wrappers, using her signature illustration style. Many friends and neighbors were sketching ideas on chocolate-stained pieces of parchment, fighting with Adobe Photoshop and Illustrator. We were working into the night to design our first original line of chocolate bar wrapping while spending long days handcrafting our dark chocolate.

We found design inspiration from everywhere—Mayan hieroglyphs, old Brooklyn tenement wallpaper, nineteenth-century textiles, trips to the Guggenheim Museum and to the docks of Cape Cod. Brooklyn is busting at the seams with world-class designers, so even trips to local boutiques, galleries, and restaurants were a source of inspiration.

Today, we are fortunate to have an incredible design team helping us. Taking a cue from the highly evolved world of wine labeling, we have decided to update our labels every year, marking each unique vintage with an original design. This strategy is not only outrageously fun, but it also keeps our design sensibilities forward-thinking and relevant, setting a new standard for how great food is packaged. —RM

CHOCOLATE HAZELNUT SPREAD

Makes 4 cups

This Italian classic can be made at home in just a few simple steps.
You won't be able to eat the store-bought stuff again. Serve on toast or with fresh fruit.

Hazelnuts	4 cups
Dark chocolate	15 ounces, finely chopped
Confectioners' sugar	1½ cups
Coconut oil	3 tablespoons

1. Preheat oven to 350 degrees Fahrenheit.
2. Roast hazelnuts on a baking sheet for 15 minutes. Let cool and then remove the skins
by rubbing within a clean kitchen towel.
3. Purée hazelnuts in a food processor until they form a paste.
4. Transfer hazelnuts to a bowl, add chocolate, confectioners' sugar, and coconut oil, and combine.
5. Purée in food processor until completely smooth.
6. Spoon into a mason jar for storage.

CHOCOLATE EGG CREAM

Serves 4

The egg cream was supposedly invented in the late nineteenth century by Brooklyn's own
Louis Auster. It is often debated whether the chocolate egg cream ever actually contained eggs.
It has never been debated as to whether or not it is crazy delicious.

CHOCOLATE SYRUP
(makes 2½ cups)

Water	2 cups
Sugar	½ cup
Cocoa powder	½ cup
Vanilla bean	Seeds scraped from ⅓ bean

EGG CREAM

Chocolate Syrup	2 cups
Whole milk	2 cups
Seltzer	2 cups

Make the Chocolate Syrup
1. In a medium saucepan, combine water, sugar, cocoa powder, and vanilla seeds and bring to a boil.
2. Take off heat and let cool.

Make the Egg Cream
3. Mix Chocolate Syrup with milk.
4. Add seltzer water. Divide among tall glasses.

FLOURLESS CHOCOLATE CAKE

Serves 8

//

Dark chocolate	1 pound, chopped
Unsalted butter	½ cup (1 stick)
Eggs	8
Granulated sugar	½ cup plus 2 tablespoons
Confectioners' sugar	2 tablespoons

//

1. Preheat oven to 350 degrees Fahrenheit. Butter an 8-inch round cake pan.
2. Melt chocolate and butter in a double boiler.
3. Separate eggs, pouring yolks into one medium bowl and whites into another.
4. Add ½ cup granulated sugar to yolks and beat until fluffy.
5. Add melted chocolate to yolk-sugar mixture.
6. Add remaining granulated sugar to egg whites and whip to form soft peaks.
7. Fold whipped egg whites into batter.
8. Pour batter into cake pan.
9. Bake for 25 minutes.
10. Sift confectioners' sugar over cooled cake.

CHOCOLATE, MAPLE & PECAN COOKIES

Makes 24

Maple sugar is becoming more widely available these days, so choose a brand that makes equally good maple syrup. We recommend Crown Maple from the Hudson River Valley. This recipe is one of our best sellers at our Williamsburg location.

Pecans	½ cup
Unsalted butter	1 cup (2 sticks), room temperature
Maple sugar	1¾ cups
Eggs	2
All-purpose flour	1¼ cups
Baking powder	1 tablespoon
Baking soda	1 teaspoon
Sea salt	1 teaspoon
Dark chocolate chips	10 ounces

1. Preheat oven to 350 degrees Fahrenheit.
2. Toast pecans on a baking sheet in oven for 10 minutes or until golden brown, and roughly chop.
3. Mix butter with maple sugar in a medium bowl.
4. Add eggs one at a time, making sure the mixture is well blended each time.
5. Add flour, baking powder and soda, salt, chopped pecans, and chocolate chips.
6. Spoon cookie dough 2 inches apart on a baking sheet using heaping tablespoons.
7. Bake for 15 minutes.

HOT CARAMEL FUDGE SAUCE

Makes 2 cups

A creamy treat, destined for the top of an ice cream sundae. Serve warm.

Sugar	½ cup
Heavy cream	1 cup
Vanilla	1 teaspoon
Dark chocolate	8 ounces, chopped

1. Cook sugar in a saucepan over medium-high heat until golden brown.
2. In a separate pot, warm cream with vanilla over medium heat.
3. Carefully pour cream into caramelized sugar and bring to a boil.
4. Stir until mixture is smooth and glossy.
5. Pour through a sieve over chocolate in a bowl and let melt.
6. Mix with spatula until smooth.

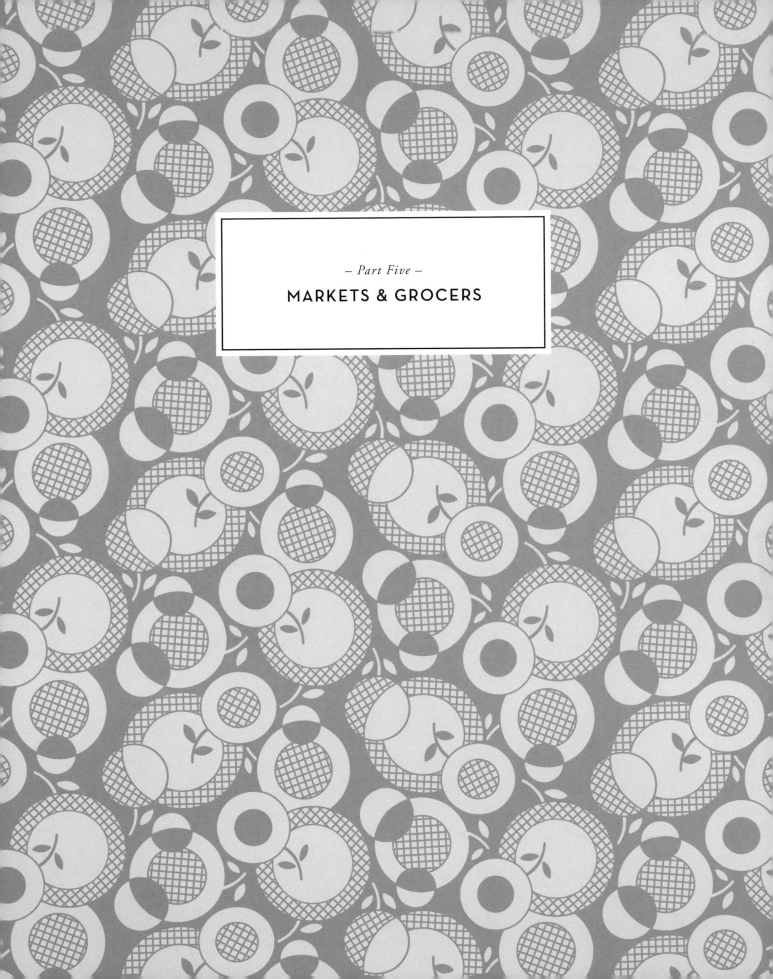

– Part Five –

MARKETS & GROCERS

GOING PUBLIC

Sourcing beans and customizing equipment was one thing; we loved experimenting and we loved making chocolate. Making chocolate for friends and family was one thing as well, but turning it into full-time work? Everyone we knew thought we were crazy. Maybe there was a reason nobody was making chocolate at the time. Many reports state that 50 percent of start-up businesses fail in the first year, and up to 90 percent fail in the first five years. Rather than be intimidated, we let these statistics drive us. It was time to introduce and sell our chocolate to strangers. We were chocolate makers first and foremost, and novice salesmen, but it was time to try. Signing up to sell at a local market in Williamsburg, we took our chocolate public.

The first Saturday market approached, and with fifty bars in a tote bag, fifty bucks in cash for change in an old cigar box, and a patterned tapestry for a tablecloth in hand, we walked up Union Avenue, under the Brooklyn-Queens Expressway, and west on North 6th Street. We were ready. "Wait, what's that?" I asked the manager at the market. "No, we didn't bring a table." Crap, off to a bad start. Luckily, someone had left theirs behind from the previous week and didn't show, so we quickly grabbed it and set up in the four-by-five-foot spot designated for us up front by the door. The Artists & Fleas market was in a hip, old, empty warehouse space with cold, broken concrete floors and white brick walls. There was no air-conditioning or heat that fall and winter, but that never caused the vendors to stay home. Extension cords and wires swung through and wrapped around the interior, making for a web of lighting anchored by power strips. The market was an incubator for emerging entrepreneurs and full of incredible craftspeople, from painters and photographers to makers of handcrafted shoes, hand-knit hats, custom jewelry, screen-printed T-shirts, and one-of-a-kind you-name-its, as well as collectors selling their rare vinyl and vintage finds and furniture. North 6th Street between Bedford Avenue and Berry Street was busy, but we were the only food makers and it was slow in the beginning. We sold just seventeen bars our first day. This was going to be more difficult than we thought. Still, we didn't get down on ourselves and celebrated with a bottle of red wine, telling our then girlfriends (now wives), Megan and Natasha, how well we did.

At the time, we knew of few other places to sell our chocolate. So we kept showing up in hopes of making enough money to pay for more beans, sugar, and rent. It was nerve-racking. There would be entire weekends when few shoppers showed up at the market. If it was raining or the weather was bad, nobody showed. If the Giants or Jets were playing, nobody showed. We still couldn't get a loan, and the credit cards were piling up and maxing out, but our stubborn passion told us we couldn't lose. We couldn't lose if people could just *taste* the chocolate. And buy it, of course.

The next Saturday we would welcome those entering the market with samples of our chocolate to taste while they walked around. Free samples? Why didn't we think of that earlier? Scrunched together by the front door, two thin, six-foot-three-inch, bearded chocolate makers with a meticulous display of seven bars with corresponding samples—people had to try our chocolate. And they did. Their eyes rolled back in delight as if tasting real chocolate for the first time. It was a much more engaging experience. We discussed our style of chocolate, introducing terms most were unfamiliar with at the time, like *bean-to-bar, single-origin,* or what *cacao percentage* referred to. Most of all, in those first days of selling and being shy around strangers, I simply wanted to get comfortable saying *cacao* (pronounced *ka-KOW*) out loud. Few people knew what it was, and it still fought my tongue when I said it.

We kept going, signing up for the new Brooklyn Flea market in Fort Greene. It felt great to introduce our chocolate in another diverse and vibrant neighborhood. Selling was hard work, but we were getting comfortable in our own skin, knowing the etiquette, rules, the subtleties of the marketplace. We were regulars at the markets by now, and our local Brooklyn neighborhoods and fellow vendors were beginning to take notice. So was a community of like-minded craftsmen. Shane Welch, founder of the local brewery Sixpoint, caught sight of what we were doing. He loved the taste of our chocolate and appreciated the home-brew relationship we had with our cacao and our vision of connecting customers to the source. So he purchased the remaining bars at our booth. Rich and I celebrated with a magnum of red wine, bought Johnny Cash's *Blue Train* LP with our hard-earned cash, and packed our empty boxes. It was the first time we were sold out of our chocolate. It wouldn't be the last. *—MM*

CHOCOLATE GRANOLA

Makes 5 cups

Throw a bag of homemade granola into your backpack, purse, or tote bag.
When you have those sudden hunger pangs, you will be glad that you did.
So will your friends if you bring enough to share.

Almonds	1 cup, roughly chopped
Pecans	1 cup, roughly chopped
Rolled oats	1 cup
Honey	½ cup
Brown sugar	2 tablespoons
Unsalted butter	3 tablespoons
Cocoa powder	2 tablespoons
Cacao nibs	½ cup
Dried cranberries	½ cup
Dark chocolate	5 ounces, chopped

1. Preheat oven to 300 degrees Fahrenheit.
2. Combine almonds, pecans, and rolled oats with honey and brown sugar.
3. Spread evenly on a baking sheet and bake for 15 minutes. Let cool.
4. Melt butter with cocoa in a saucepan.
5. Mix together cacao nibs, cranberries, and the roasted mixture.
6. Stir in the melted butter mixture.
7. Mix in the chopped dark chocolate.

CHOCOLATE ROLL

Serves 8

////////////////////////////////////

CAKE

Eggs	4
Granulated sugar	1 cup
All-purpose flour	¾ cup
Potato starch	¼ cup
Cocoa powder	¼ cup
Baking powder	1½ teaspoons

FILLING

Unsalted butter	½ cup (1 stick), room temperature
Confectioners' sugar	1½ cups
Cream cheese	8 ounces

////////////////////////////////////

Make the Cake

1. Preheat oven to 375 degrees Fahrenheit. Butter and flour a baking sheet.
2. In a medium bowl, whisk eggs and granulated sugar until fluffy.
3. Sift flour, potato starch, cocoa powder, and baking powder and gently fold them into eggs.
4. Spread the batter ¼ inch thick on the baking sheet.
5. Bake for 10 minutes.
6. Place kitchen towel on top of cake and flip upside down on counter.
7. Roll up cake from a short edge while still warm. Let cool.

Make the Filling

8. Cream butter with confectioners' sugar until fluffy.
9. Combine cream cheese with butter-sugar mixture and mix until smooth.

Assemble

10. Unroll cake.
11. Spread filling evenly over cake.
12. Roll cake back up.
13. Cut into 1-inch slices to reveal spiral filling pattern.

MARBLED CHEESECAKE BROWNIES

Makes 16

If you're having trouble marbling in the cream cheese,
whip the cream cheese with a bit of heavy cream.

Dark chocolate	12 ounces, chopped
Unsalted butter	¾ cup (1½ sticks)
Brown sugar	1½ cups
Vanilla bean	Seeds scraped from 1 bean
Eggs	5
All-purpose flour	½ cup
Baking powder	1 teaspoon
Sea salt	1 teaspoon
Cream cheese	4 ounces, whipped

1. Preheat oven to 325 degrees Fahrenheit. Butter an 8-inch square baking pan.
2. Melt the chocolate, butter, and brown sugar in a saucepan over low heat.
3. Add vanilla seeds to mixture.
4. Add the eggs and combine.
5. Add flour, baking powder, and salt and combine until smooth.
6. Gently fold in a quarter of the cream cheese at a time, leaving marbled effect.
7. Pour marbled batter into baking pan.
8. Bake for 40 minutes. Let cool.
9. Cut into 2-inch squares.

RASPBERRY ROSE CHOCOLATE TART

Serves 10

///

CRUST

All-purpose flour	2½ cups
Sugar	3 tablespoons
Unsalted butter	1 cup (2 sticks)
Egg yolks	2
Ice water	¼ cup

GANACHE

Heavy cream	1 cup
Dark chocolate	8 ounces, chopped
Unsalted butter	5 tablespoons, room temperature
Rose water	4½ teaspoons

TOPPING

Fresh raspberries	2 cups

///

Make the Crust

1. Preheat oven to 350 degrees Fahrenheit.
2. In the bowl of a standing mixer, mix flour, sugar, and butter until flaky.
3. Add egg yolks and ice water and mix until dough forms.
4. Turn dough out onto work surface and knead by hand until smooth.
5. Wrap dough in plastic wrap and let rest in refrigerator for 30 minutes.
6. Roll out dough to roughly ⅛-inch thickness to fit into a 12-inch tart pan.
7. Bake for 20 minutes. Let cool.

Make the Ganache

8. Bring cream to a boil. Pour over chocolate in a heatproof bowl.
9. Let sit and melt for 2 minutes.
10. Whisk in tight circles from the center outward until emulsified.
11. Add butter and rose water and stir.

Assemble

12. Pour ganache into cooled crust and let set for 2 hours.
13. Cover tart with fresh raspberries. Serve chilled.

PEANUT NIB BRITTLE

Makes 2 pounds

When caramelizing the sugar, water, and honey, combine but do not stir.

Sugar	2 cups
Water	½ cup
Honey	½ cup
Cacao nibs	½ cup
Peanuts	½ cup
Unsalted butter	2 tablespoons
Baking soda	1 teaspoon
Sea salt	1 teaspoon

1. Combine sugar, water, and honey in a saucepan.
2. Bring mixture to a simmer and cook until golden brown. Take off heat.
3. Add nibs, peanuts, butter, and baking soda. Mixture will foam.
4. Stir until fully combined.
5. Pour hot mixture onto a rimmed baking sheet.
6. Sprinkle salt over brittle.
7. Let cool and break into pieces.

CHOCOLATE DATE CAKE

Serves 8

Garnish the top of the cake with chopped dates and pecans.

///

Water	2 cups
Baking soda	2 teaspoons
Dates	1 pound
Unsalted butter	¾ cup (1½ sticks), room temperature
Sugar	1 cup
Egg	1
All-purpose flour	2 cups
Sea salt	½ teaspoon
Dark chocolate	1 pound, chopped
Pecans	½ cup chopped

///

1. Bring water to a boil with baking soda.
2. Add dates, remove from heat, and soak for 30 minutes.
3. Preheat oven to 375 degrees Fahrenheit. Butter a 9-inch round cake pan.
4. In a medium bowl, cream butter with sugar until fluffy.
5. Add egg, flour, and salt and combine.
6. Drain dates.
7. Add drained dates, chocolate, and pecans.
8. Pour batter into cake pan.
9. Bake for 30 minutes. Serve warm.

IT TAKES A VILLAGE

Our goal was to make delicious chocolate for our friends, family, and community, and to support our community by being their chocolate maker of choice. Brooklyn had cheese and butcher shops, woodworkers, beekeepers, local breweries, and pickle makers, but no local chocolate maker. We knew it was going to take a village to help us on our journey and to share our vision and, most important, our chocolate with those in the neighborhood.

We used local ingredients for tasty additions to our chocolate, even including foraged walnuts from Central Park in limited-run bars. We gave back to the community and, with a focus on zero waste, donated the cacao shells (or husks) to Rooftop Farms, Brooklyn Grange, and the Brooklyn Botanic Garden for mulch. The more we gave, the happier people were, and the happier we were. And it came full circle. Eventually, a true local supporter got word of our chocolate and helped us take our small business to the next level.

After many months of selling at the Artists & Fleas market in Williamsburg and the Brooklyn Flea in Fort Greene, we had our first big bite. George Vitray, who managed Spuyten Duyvil, a small craft beer and microbrewery shop, bought one of each of our bars to share with his boss, Joe Carrol. Joe was a musician who loved microbreweries and craft beer. He and his wife decided to start a bar below their apartment on Metropolitan Avenue, which was basically a living room for them at the time. They served unique beers from small corners of the world alongside carefully selected meats, cheeses, and pickles. George and Joe sampled our bars and said that "it was like eating chocolate for the first time."

The next day I got a call from Joe. He was interested in purchasing a case of each, twelve varieties at that time. While on the phone, I glanced over at our inven-

tory and calculated maybe a couple dozen bars sitting on a small wire rack in my bedroom. He wanted the bars on his shelves and got straight to the point: "How many bars are in a case?"

A case? We only sell bars at the moment, I thought to myself. "About, um, thirty," I replied.

"How much per case?" Joe asked.

"Well, let's see, we sell them for seven dollars, so. . . ." I stuttered since I hadn't quite thought through any sort of wholesale pricing at this stage in our business.

"Just make sure you cover your costs but set a lower price for wholesale than your retail, and let me know," he advised. Got it, I nodded to myself. Wholesale is less than retail but greater than cost. Brilliant. Sure, I held an honors degree in economics, but we were simply testing our first batches and didn't realize the demand could spark so early.

We now had our first wholesale account. Rick and I would stop by the shop, checking in on our bars as if they had gone off to school. George would gregariously greet us, offering samples of exclusive, rare, and delicious beers and ciders. With Joe's support and George's enthusiasm, Spuyten Duyvil led the way for other huge local supporters in the neighborhood, including Marlow & Sons, the Bedford Cheese Shop, Stinky Brooklyn (also a cheese shop), and the Park Slope Food Coop, the oldest co-op in the United States. With those few first accounts, we couldn't keep up with orders. Joe came into our new factory on North 3rd Street for a tour to see how everything was going. He wanted more chocolate and we were unable to deliver without delays. We were sorting, cracking, and winnowing by hand, grinding in small-batch, forty-pound wet grinders whose motors, gears, and belts we had customized, before aging the chocolate for thirty days

or more. But none of those areas were our bottleneck; we were still tempering ten pounds at a time with our countertop units, and hand-ladling the liquid chocolate into molds, before banging it on the counters so that the bars would even out and air bubbles would rise to the top. At one point, we even tried using an old electronic football game as our vibrating table for that final stage. We needed help.

It was 2009, and we were still in the eye of the storm of the financial crisis, had not been able to get a traditional loan with a bank, and simply continued to max out credit cards. Joe offered to help. The banks weren't offering great returns on his money, and he was a huge supporter of local visionaries. He asked what it would take to keep bars on his shelves. We needed a proper tempering machine. But it came with a hefty price tag.

"How much?" he asked. We told him the amount.

"No problem," he casually replied.

We couldn't believe this was real. We promised to pay it back within one year in a simple one-paragraph contract. Joe brought a check the next day. It was an unbelievable display of encouragement, trust, and vision on his part. I'm not sure if he got the consent of his lawyer

or accountant, or his wife for that matter. Judging by his simple contract, I imagine he didn't, which was another reason we were drawn to Joe and his independent spirit. Communities were based on trust. That and hoping you wouldn't get your legs broken.

A few months passed and we hadn't paid back a dime. We had credit cards accumulating interest with APRs jumping from 0 to 17 percent. It was summer, sales were slow, and we didn't have air-conditioning. We promised big checks to come with the holidays on the horizon, and Joe was patient but getting understandably nervous. Time passed. The sales finally came. I rode my bike to Spuyten Duyvil with the final check, including interest, and knocked on the closed door. Nobody was there. I wrote a note and tossed it in the mailbox outside. We had kept our promise and paid him back just under the wire.

Joe and Spuyten Duyvil, and our first accounts and supporters—Andrew Tarlow at Marlow & Sons, Stinky Brooklyn, Bedford Cheese Shop, and the community at Park Slope Food Coop—will always remind us that nobody starts a company on their own. It really does take a village, and we stand on the shoulders of giants, these giant supporters of our local community. —*MM*

CHOCOLATE BREAD PUDDING

Serves 8

This is our idea of comfort food. Crunchy on the outside and custardy on the inside.

Raisins	½ cup
Brandy	½ cup
Whole milk	3 cups
Eggs	8
Sugar	1 cup
Ground cinnamon	2 tablespoons
Brioche	1 loaf (1½ pounds)
Dark chocolate	5 ounces
Unsalted butter	¼ cup (½ stick), cut into ¼-inch slices

1. Soak the raisins in the brandy for at least 1 hour.
2. In a large bowl, whisk together milk, eggs, sugar, and cinnamon.
3. Cut brioche into ½-inch slices. Dip into milk-egg mixture.
4. Chop chocolate into fine pieces.
5. Place soaked brioche slices in a standard loaf pan.
6. Drain and sprinkle brandied raisins, chocolate, and butter between the layers.
7. Pour milk-egg mixture over brioche.
8. Cover and refrigerate for 2 hours.
9. Preheat oven to 350 degrees Fahrenheit.
10. Bake for 1 hour.

CHOCOLATE STRAWBERRY SHORTCAKE

Serves 8

Garnish shortcake with chocolate fudge sauce and fresh mint.

///

SHORTCAKE

All-purpose flour	1½ cups
Baking powder	1 tablespoon
Baking soda	½ teaspoon
Sea salt	½ teaspoon
Unsalted butter	⅓ cup (a little over 5 tablespoons)
Dark chocolate	1 ounce, chopped
Sugar	½ cup
Buttermilk	1 cup

FILLING

Heavy cream	2 cups
Fresh strawberries	1 pound

///

Make the Shortcake

1. Preheat oven to 375 degrees Fahrenheit.
2. In a food processor, mix flour, baking powder and soda, and salt together.
3. Cut butter into small cubes and mix with dry ingredients.
4. Melt chocolate, sugar, and buttermilk in a double boiler.
5. Combine wet and dry mixtures and stir until batter is smooth.
6. Pour batter into a 9-inch round cake pan.
7. Bake for 20 minutes.

Make the Filling

8. In the bowl of a standing mixer or in a medium bowl using a handheld mixer, whip cream to soft peaks.
9. Cut strawberries into quarters.

Assemble

10. Slice cake horizontally in half.
11. Spread whipped cream and strawberries between cake layers.
12. Garnish with more whipped cream and strawberries.

SOUR CREAM FUDGE CAKE

Serves 8

Garnish with shaved chocolate and cacao nibs.

//

CAKE

Unsalted butter	1 cup (2 sticks), room temperature
Granulated sugar	2 cups
Egg yolks	3
Cake flour	2½ cups
Cocoa powder	3 tablespoons
Sour cream	1 cup
Water	½ cup
Baking soda	1 teaspoon

FROSTING

Sour cream	1 cup
Confectioners' sugar	1 cup
Heavy cream	1 cup

//

Make the Cake

1. Preheat oven to 350 degrees Fahrenheit. Butter a 9-inch round cake pan.
2. In a medium bowl, cream butter with granulated sugar until fluffy.
3. Add egg yolks and combine.
4. Add flour, cocoa powder, and sour cream and combine.
5. Bring water to a boil and mix with baking soda.
6. Add water mixture to batter and stir.
7. Pour the batter into the cake pan.
8. Bake for 35 minutes. Let cool.

Make the Frosting

9. In the bowl of a standing mixer, combine all of the ingredients and mix until smooth.

Assemble

10. Spread frosting on top of cake.

CHOCOLATE MERINGUE PIE

Serves 10

As fun to make as it is to eat.
Prepare to receive a standing ovation after dinner tonight.

///

CRUST

All-purpose flour	2 cups
Cocoa powder	½ cup
Granulated sugar	3 tablespoons
Unsalted butter	1 cup (2 sticks), room temperature and cubed
Egg yolks	2
Ice water	¼ cup

GANACHE

Heavy cream	1 cup
Dark chocolate	7½ ounces, chopped
Unsalted butter	5 tablespoons

MERINGUE

Egg whites	6 (1 cup)
Confectioners' sugar	2 cups

///

Make the Crust
1. Preheat oven to 350 degrees Fahrenheit.
2. In the bowl of a standing mixer, combine flour, cocoa powder, granulated sugar, and butter until flaky.
3. Add egg yolks and ice water. Mix until doughy.
4. Turn dough out onto work surface and knead by hand until smooth.
5. Wrap dough in plastic wrap and let rest in refrigerator for 30 minutes.
6. Roll out dough to fit in the bottom and up the sides of a 12-inch pie plate.
7. Bake crust for 20 minutes. Let cool.

Make the Ganache

8. In a saucepan, bring cream to a boil.

9. Pour cream over chocolate in a heatproof bowl.

10. Let it sit and melt for 1 minute.

11. Stir with a spatula in tight circles from the center outward.

12. Cool to 108 degrees Fahrenheit. Test with an instant-read thermometer.

13. Add butter and combine until fully incorporated.

14. Pour ganache over cooled piecrust.

15. Refrigerate for 2 hours.

Make the Meringue

16. In the clean bowl of a standing mixer, whip egg whites to soft peaks.

17. Add confectioners' sugar and mix until glossy.

18. Cover the pie with the meringue. Brown peaks with a kitchen blowtorch.

BUTCHERS

I dream of a time when every neighborhood has a chocolate maker. The world's most popular food in the hands of a trusted member of the community, who advises customers on origin, tasting notes, recipes, and applications. Chocolate varieties available by the pound behind glass displays. "A quarter pound of the San Martin and a half pound of the smoked Papua New Guinea, please." Recipe cards on the counter to take home, a familiar, smiling face, and out-of-this-world aromas greeting you as you enter. Chocolate makers wearing pressed white chef's jackets and stained aprons cutting untempered, single-estate blocks of chocolate, weighing them out on a hanging scale, and wrapping them in butcher paper. Freshly baked cookies, brownies, and carefully rolled confections sitting next to the register.

Sound familiar? The scene I've conjured describes the Mast Brothers factory and retail operation in Williamsburg, Brooklyn, fairly accurately. But the original model for our vision was the traditional butcher shop. We love butcher shops. The McFaddens of Staubitz, Tom Mylan of Meat Hook, Fleisher's, and the whole gang at Marlow & Daughters are part of a century-long tradition of Brooklyn butchers that is growing stronger than ever.

How does a butcher inspire a chocolate maker? A butcher's role in the community is vital. To walk into your local butcher shop is to embrace the importance of neighborly trust. Anonymity, as is often the experience at the meat counter in large supermarkets, fosters disconnection and, often, bad decisions. The larger the role your butcher plays in your life, the more respect you have for each other and, therefore, the more care goes into ingredient selection, cut, and recommendations.

A butcher shop connects the customer to the source—the nearby farms, farmers, and slaughterhouse—and thus humanizes the process. This draws attention to what we call the human scale of the business. Often critiqued as overly precious or unsustainable, the human scale doesn't simply glorify small or cute; it glorifies *human*. It glorifies our unique ability to decide *should* over *could*. It allows us to calculate sustainability using dollars and sense.

A butcher shop defines its success in terms of craft and tradition. Your local butcher prospers when he or she becomes more efficient, trimming cleaner, but also when the customer is engaged, informed, and made to feel comfortable.

Who would have thought that preparing and selling chocolate and preparing and selling meat could have so much in common? Outside the shop, chocolate can go beautifully with a wide variety of meats, in dry rubs, sauces, and seasonings. So the next time you are at your local butcher shop, make sure you head to your local chocolate maker on your way home. —*RM*

STEAK WITH NIBS & PEPPERCORNS

Makes 2 large steaks

Talk to your local butcher and see what cut is recommended.
My butcher says a nice thick rib eye will do the trick.

//

Black peppercorns	2 tablespoons
Red peppercorns	2 tablespoons
Green peppercorns	2 tablespoons
Cacao nibs	2 tablespoons
Sea salt	1 tablespoon
Steaks	2 (24-ounce) rib eyes, or cut of your choice, room temperature

//

1. Preheat oven to 325 degrees Fahrenheit.
2. Roast all peppercorns on a baking sheet for 10 minutes.
3. Crush peppercorns lightly with cacao nibs in a mortar with a pestle.
4. Add salt to mixture.
5. Spread rub over both sides of steaks.
6. Sear steaks on both sides for a dark-crust exterior and medium-rare interior.

COCOA DRY RUB

Makes about 1 pint; seasons 1 large rack
of ribs, 4 steaks, or the equivalent

Store your rub in a mason jar and use year-round.

Brown sugar	½ cup
Cacao nibs	½ cup, ground
Cocoa powder	¼ cup
Paprika	¼ cup
Black pepper	1 tablespoon
Chili powder	1 tablespoon
Garlic powder	1 tablespoon
Onion powder	1 tablespoon
Cayenne pepper	1 teaspoon

1. Whisk together all ingredients in a medium bowl.
2. Store in an airtight container.
3. Use for any kind of meat.

CACAO NIB SALAD

Serves 8

Think of cacao nibs as more nuts than chocolate.
This savory garnish provides beautiful texture to a simple and refreshing salad.

Arugula	1 bunch
Frisée	1 bunch
Baby spinach	1 bunch
Dill	4 sprigs
Basil	4 sprigs
Cocoa Balsamic Vinaigrette (page 235)	½ cup
Cacao nibs	½ cup
Blood orange	1
Orange	1
Sea salt	½ tablespoon
Black pepper	½ tablespoon

1. Tear the greens and herbs into bite-size pieces.
2. Toss in a large bowl with Cocoa Balsamic Vinaigrette.
3. Add cacao nibs.
4. Peel and slice and add oranges.
5. Toss with salt and pepper.

CACAO COUNTRY PÂTÉ

Serves 10

Imagine coming home after a long day's work to find a nice board of pâté and cheeses waiting for you. Cacao nibs give this rustic pâté incredible texture.

Unsalted butter	¼ cup (½ stick)
Yellow onion	1 medium, finely chopped
Garlic	3 cloves, minced
Cognac	½ cup
Fresh thyme	1 tablespoon
Ground allspice	2 teaspoons
Lardo (ask your butcher)	8 ounces
Ground pork	2 pounds
Eggs	2
Sea salt	4 teaspoons
Black pepper	1 teaspoon
Cacao nibs	1 cup
Bacon	1 pound

1. Preheat oven to 300 degrees Fahrenheit.
2. Melt butter in a saucepan.
3. Sauté onion and garlic until translucent.
4. Add Cognac, thyme, and allspice and reduce by half.
5. Set aside and let cool.
6. Cut *lardo* into small cubes and add to ground pork in a large bowl.
7. Add eggs and reduction to pork mixture and combine.
8. Season with salt and pepper.
9. Add cacao nibs and combine.
10. Line a 5-by-9-by-3-inch loaf pan with bacon, letting ends overhang.
11. Press pâté mixture into pan.
12. Fold bacon slices over, covering the pâté.
13. Bake until interior reaches 155 degrees Fahrenheit. Test with an instant-read thermometer.
14. Let cool. Cut into 1-inch slices.

CHOCOLATE BARBECUE SAUCE

Makes about 3 cups

This dark, rich, and spicy sauce is perfect for a brisk day of tailgating.
Serve with roasted, grilled, or fried meats.

Unsalted butter	2 tablespoons
Garlic	5 cloves, minced
Red onion	1 medium, chopped
Tomatoes	4, diced
Habanero chile	½, diced
Ground cumin	1 teaspoon
Ground cinnamon	1 teaspoon
Chili powder	½ teaspoon
Sherry vinegar	½ cup
Brown sugar	¼ cup
Chicken stock	2 cups
Brewed espresso	2 tablespoons
Dark chocolate	2½ ounces, chopped
Sea salt	2 teaspoons
Black pepper	2 teaspoons

1. Melt butter over medium heat in a saucepan.
2. Add garlic and onion and sauté until golden brown.
3. Add tomatoes and habanero chile.
4. Cook down for 5 minutes.
5. Add cumin, cinnamon, and chili powder and stir.
6. Add vinegar and sugar.
7. Reduce to a paste-like consistency.
8. Add chicken stock and espresso.
9. Simmer for 30 minutes.
10. Add chocolate and combine until smooth.
11. Season with salt and pepper.

CINCINNATI CHILI

Serves 8

Found at chili parlors throughout Ohio.
We often serve this with noodles and shredded cheese.

//

Vegetable oil	2 tablespoons
Yellow onion	1 medium, finely chopped
Ground beef	2 pounds
Chili powder	¼ cup
Ground cumin	1 teaspoon
Ground allspice	1 teaspoon
Ground cloves	½ teaspoon
Bay leaves	2
Cayenne pepper	¼ teaspoon
Tomato purée	1½ cups
Beef stock	4 cups
Dark chocolate	2½ ounces, chopped
Sherry vinegar	2 tablespoons
Sea salt	2 pinches
Black pepper	2 pinches

//

1. In a large pot, heat vegetable oil and sauté onion over medium heat until translucent.
2. Add ground beef and cook until browned.
3. Stir in chili powder, cumin, allspice, cloves, bay leaves, cayenne, and tomato purée.
4. Cover and let simmer for 20 minutes.
5. Add beef stock. Let simmer, uncovered, for 1 hour.
6. Add chocolate and vinegar and combine.
7. Remove bay leaves. Season with salt and pepper.

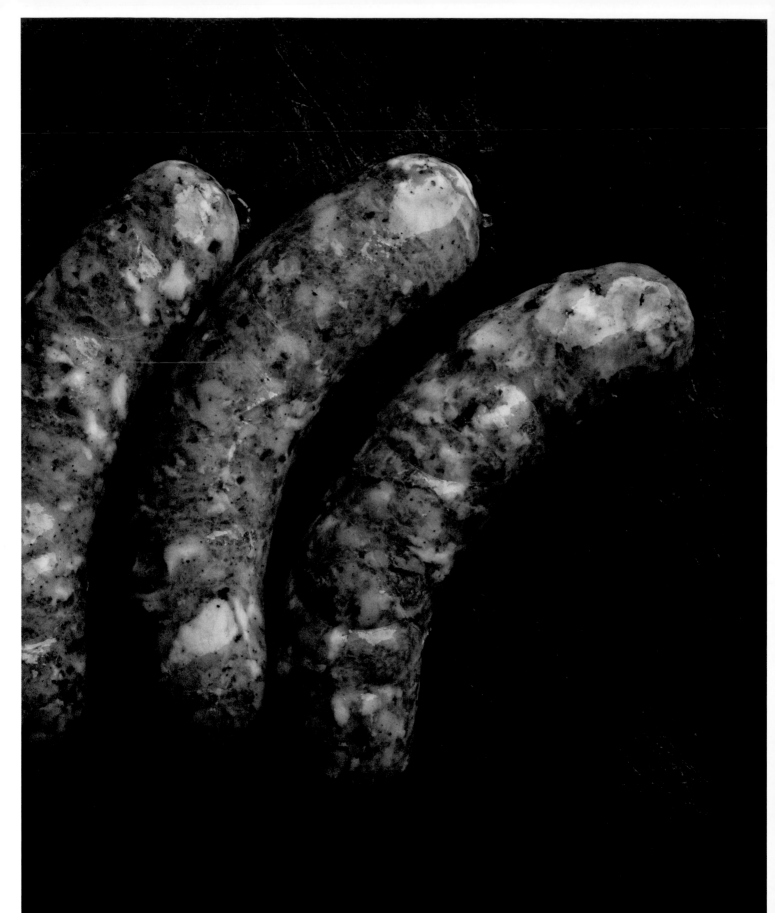

CACAO NIB PORK SAUSAGE

Makes 10

Even with the cacao nibs, this sausage remains beautifully savory.
Try it paired with kale in an all-day-simmering soup, or on its own for breakfast.

Yellow onion	1 medium, finely diced
Garlic	2 cloves, minced
Fresh thyme	1 tablespoon
Fresh sage	1½ teaspoons
Cayenne pepper	¼ teaspoon
Ground pork butt	2 pounds
Smoked bacon	¼ cup chopped into ½-inch cubes
Cacao nibs	½ cup
Sea salt	2 teaspoons
Black pepper	1 teaspoon
Hog casings	10

1. Combine onion and garlic with thyme, sage, cayenne, and ground pork in a large bowl.
2. Add bacon to mixture.
3. Add cacao nibs.
4. Season with salt and pepper.
5. Stuff hog casings with mixture.
6. Cook sausages in grill pan until evenly browned.

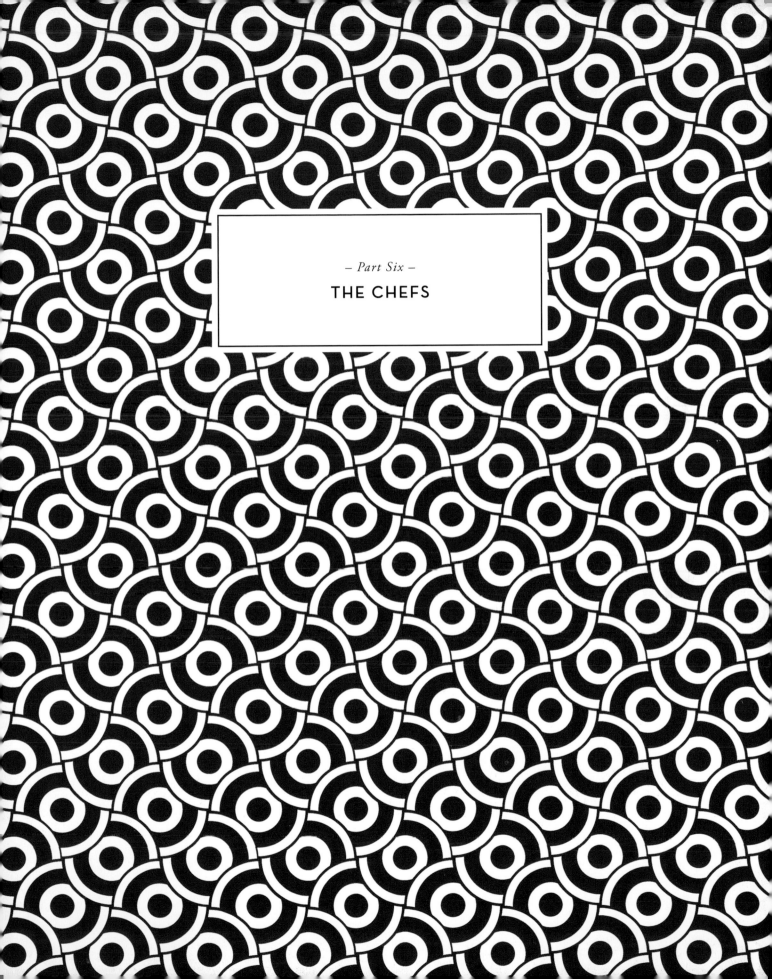

– Part Six –

THE CHEFS

A SURPRISE VISITOR

*T*he Christmas season was upon us. My brother and I were in early and home late, very late. We had been known to stay until 3 or 4 a.m. and be back at it the following day at 8 a.m. to get the holiday chocolate orders out. We found ourselves turning away customer after customer, even putting a "Sold Out" sign on our front door in December! Orders were stacking up and we were falling weeks behind. The Park Slope Food Coop alone was ordering more than 3,000 chocolate bars a week! We couldn't believe it, but our adrenaline and perfectionism (and lots of coffee) kept us focused as we tempered bar after bar, sprinkling almonds, sea salt, and cranberries in a disciplined dance. When the chocolate was in perfect temper, it was time to go get it. Clean the cooling cabinets, clean the molds, measure the chocolate, add ingredients, into the cabinet, and repeat.

"Excuse me, brothers," said Arto, then our apprentice, now in sales. "There is a Chef Thomas Keller to see you two," he announced with a smirk. My brother and I stared at each other, quickly determining whether we could abandon our rigorous system. Yes, we could. The last mold of the session was in our grasp. We hurriedly exited the tempering room and headed to the storefront. Looking like two surgeons excited to break the good news, we stripped off our latex gloves in mid-stride.

"Hi, Chef, welcome to the factory!" Equally exhausted and excited, my heart raced as I reached my hand out to shake his hand for the first time. He was immaculately dressed, in a perfectly tailored dark wool overcoat with a crisp red scarf. "I've been doing some Christmas shopping and wanted to stop by and see your factory before I head to the airport back to Napa Valley. Let me introduce you to our chef at French Laundry, Cory Lee." The French Laundry had already begun using our chocolate on occasion, but I am and always will be a chef at heart and was honored and speechless to meet them both.

Although we had eaten at Per Se and spoken to his staff there about our craft, I knew this was the encounter I'd remember forever. I couldn't wait to overwhelm him with our professionalism, seriousness, and sense of duty. I glanced quickly over at Michael and realized we both had our beard nets on and looked ridiculous.

In the industry they are often referred to as "snoods." I know I sure felt like a snood. Sure, they are a necessity for kitchen work, but let's admit it, they look ridiculous. Like a fisherman's net covering a face full of cod.

I laughed it off, making a joke about how he'd probably never let us in his kitchen with beards like these. He calmed our nerves with an accepting smile, looked to the rest of our factory, and told us how impressed and proud he was of us and our operation.

I was walking on air and talking a mile a minute as I discussed the simplicity of our process, our focus on sourcing great ingredients, and how much he had inspired us in the way we make chocolate. His restaurants are an inspiration and use dozens of pounds of our chocolate a week! Our relationship with both Per Se and French Laundry (not to mention Bouchon) is special and we cherish it. It is built on mutual respect and a passion for the uncompromised best. —*RM*

CHOCOLATE SOUFFLÉ

Serves 4

The soufflé has an undeservedly notorious reputation—do not be intimidated!

///

Dark chocolate	7½ ounces, chopped
Unsalted butter	¼ cup (½ stick), plus more for coating ramekins
Egg yolks	3
Sugar	½ cup plus 2 tablespoons
Water	3 tablespoons
Egg whites	8

///

1. Preheat oven to 375 degrees Fahrenheit.
2. Melt chocolate and butter together in a double boiler.
3. In a separate bowl, using a handheld mixer, beat egg yolks, 2 tablespoons sugar, and water to a froth.
4. Combine both mixtures and whisk until emulsified.
5. In a separate bowl, using a handheld mixer, beat egg whites and ¼ cup sugar to soft peaks.
6. Add remaining sugar and beat on high speed to hold stiff peaks.
7. Working quickly, fold one-third of the egg whites into the chocolate mixture.
8. Fold in the remaining egg whites to form a smooth mixture.
9. Brush individual ramekins with soft butter and coat them with additional sugar.
10. Fill ramekins three-quarters full with the soufflé mixture.
11. Bake for 15 minutes or until fully risen.

COCOA COQ AU VIN

Serves 4

///

MARINADE

Onion	1 medium
Garlic	3 cloves
Cacao nibs	½ cup
Cocoa powder	1 tablespoon
Red wine	½ (750 ml) bottle
Whole chicken	1 (4 pounds)

COQ AU VIN

Onion	1 medium
Garlic	3 cloves
Celery	4 stalks
Carrots	2
Pancetta	4 ounces
Unsalted butter	2 tablespoons
All-purpose flour	2 tablespoons
Tomato paste	3 tablespoons
Mushrooms	8 ounces (morels and/or champignons)
Red wine	1 (750 ml) bottle
Chicken stock	4 cups
Cacao nibs	1 cup
Dark chocolate	1 ounce, chopped
Cocoa powder	1 tablespoon
Fresh thyme	1 teaspoon
Bay leaves	2
Sea salt	1 teaspoon
Black pepper	1 teaspoon

///

Make the Marinade

1. Chop onion and garlic.

2. Add cacao nibs, cocoa powder, and red wine.

3. Put chicken in large ziplock bag with marinade.

4. Refrigerate overnight (or 2 hours minimum).

Make the Coq au Vin

5. Preheat oven to 400 degrees Fahrenheit.

6. Roughly chop onion, garlic, celery, and carrots. Set celery and carrots aside.

7. Cut pancetta into small cubes.

8. In a large stockpot over medium heat, sweat onion and garlic in butter until translucent.

9. Add pancetta and cook until lightly browned.

10. Add flour and stir.

11. Add carrots, celery, and tomato paste and stir.

12. Add mushrooms and red wine and stir.

13. Reduce by half. Add chicken stock, nibs, chocolate, cocoa powder, thyme,
bay leaves, salt, and pepper and stir.

14. Add marinated chicken.

15. Place pot, uncovered, in oven for 20 minutes.

16. Lower oven temperature to 325 degrees Fahrenheit.

17. Cook for 1 more hour.

CHOCOLATE POTS DE CRÈME

Serves 4

//

Whole milk	2 cups
Heavy cream	1 cup
Vanilla bean	Seeds scraped from 1 bean
Eggs	6
Sugar	½ cup
Dark chocolate	5 ounces, chopped

//

1. Preheat oven to 200 degrees Fahrenheit.
2. In a saucepan, combine milk and cream with vanilla seeds. Bring to boil, and take off heat.
3. In a medium bowl, combine eggs and sugar.
4. Pour hot milk mixture over chocolate in a heatproof bowl and let sit for 2 minutes.
5. Mix until smooth.
6. Combine chocolate mixture with egg-sugar mixture and stir until smooth.
7. Pour into individual ramekins.
8. Bake for 30 minutes, until set.

ORANGE NIB-CRUSTED SALMON

Serves 4

The versatility of the cacao nib is on display as its incredible texture, acidity, and nuttiness
create a savory crust for the fish. Garnish with dill and croutons. Serve with baby spinach leaves or watercress.

///

SAUCE

Unsalted butter	½ cup (1 stick)
White wine vinegar	2 tablespoons
Egg yolks	2
Sea salt	1 teaspoon

SPICE RUB

Cacao nibs	¼ cup
Orange zest	1 tablespoon
Whole cloves	1 tablespoon
Sea salt	2 teaspoons
Black pepper	2 teaspoons

SALMON

Wild salmon	1 pound
Sea salt	1½ teaspoons
Black pepper	1½ teaspoons
Extra-virgin olive oil	1 tablespoon

///

Make the Sauce

1. Put butter in a small saucepan over medium heat and cook until golden brown.

2. Let cool to room temperature.

3. In a medium bowl, whisk vinegar, egg yolks, and salt to combine.

4. Slowly add brown butter, whisking until emulsified.

5. Keep at room temperature.

Make the Spice Rub
6. Put all of the ingredients in a mortar and grind them with a pestle to a fine paste. Set aside.

Make the Salmon
7. Preheat oven to 250 degrees Fahrenheit.
8. Cut salmon into 4 equal fillets.
9. Season with salt and pepper.
10. Rub spice mixture onto salmon (set a bit aside for garnish).
11. Heat a cast-iron skillet with olive oil over high heat.
12. Sear salmon until crispy.
13. Finish in oven for 5 minutes for medium-rare.

BLACK TRUFFLE TRUFFLES

Makes 24

Take your Valentine's Day treat to the next level by
adding pure decadence to an already decadent confection.

//

GANACHE

Heavy cream	½ cup
Dark chocolate	5 ounces, chopped
Unsalted butter	2 tablespoons, room temperature
Black truffle oil	1 teaspoon

COATING

Dark chocolate	10 ounces, melted and tempered (see page 9)
Cocoa powder	½ cup

//

Make the Ganache

1. Bring cream to a boil in a saucepan over medium-high heat.
2. Pour cream over chocolate in a heatproof bowl.
3. Let sit and melt for 1 minute.
4. Using a spatula, stir in tight circles from the center outward.
5. Allow mixture to cool to 108 degrees Fahrenheit. Test with an instant-read thermometer.
6. Add butter and stir until combined.
7. Add truffle oil and stir until combined.
8. Shape ganache into marble-size spheres by rolling between your hands.

Coat the Truffles

9. Dip in tempered chocolate.
10. Roll in cocoa powder, and cool until set.

FIRST BEST MEAL

⁄⁄⁄⁄⁄⁄⁄⁄

*O*ur bags were full of our single-origin chocolate. Rick and I jumped on the subway to Grand Central and then ran to catch Metro North heading up the Hudson to Tarrytown. The train ride along the river is magnificent, with the high cliffs of the Palisades hugging the river to the west. We were giddy with excitement, because we were on our way to meet with another brother duo, Dan and David Barber, who take the farm-to-table mantra very seriously at their restaurant Blue Hill at Stone Barns.

Exiting at Tarrytown, we grabbed a cab and wound through the town of Sleepy Hollow before reaching Bedford Road and turning onto the long drive that would take us up to Stone Barns. On either side of the drive were free-roaming chickens; pigs and cows were up over the hill; a large greenhouse sat in the valley west of the main building. We got out of the cab and walked through gardens and into the courtyard of the attached structures. We were transported to another world. Were we in southern France or a small Italian village? I'd never been to either, but we certainly weren't in Brooklyn anymore.

David Barber approached us with an outstretched hand in the courtyard and proceeded to give us a tour of the small café, grounds, expanding greenhouse, and farm animals. We headed back around the courtyard and into the restaurant for a tour of Blue Hill's immaculate kitchen and to meet his brother, the head chef at Stone Barns, Dan Barber. Dan greeted us with a big smile, showed us around the various prep stations in action, and escorted us to an adjacent back patio.

"We'll grab the entire staff and meet out here," Dan said.

"Sounds great," I said, a hollow feeling in my stomach. This was the first time we had ever spoken to the kitchen staff at a restaurant. I figured maybe we'd sit around a workstation with five or six chefs, then taste and talk about our chocolate. I figured wrong. Dan and David came out with about sixty of their crew, fanning out around the patio and into the benches of the farmhouse picnic tables. The chefs and cooks in their whites, waitstaff and hosts in their aprons, and anyone and everyone who worked at the cafés or elsewhere were standing by, attentively.

At the time, I had a tendency to go blank when asked to speak in front of a large group. Standing front and center, I whispered to Rick, "You got this, right?" "I was planning on it," he replied. We spoke for about forty-five minutes, discussing where chocolate comes from, how it's made, our passion, our vision for locally produced craft chocolate.

They recognized that what we were doing was new. It was different. Nobody had tasted chocolate like ours—no dumbing down of the flavors with added butters, vanilla, or emulsifiers; on the contrary, we highlighted the magnificent citrus, berry, tobacco, banana, cinnamon, plum, even earthy notes of cacao from various regions. Blue Hill's menu was driven by ingredients sourced from their gardens and from the Barber family's farm in western Massachusetts. The meat and poultry were from animals raised on the eighty acres of field and pasture at Stone Barns. Their wines were selected to complement, harmonize, and highlight the seasonal products and dishes. The Barbers and their staff were no strangers to the nuances and subtleties of high-quality ingredients and food produced with attention and passion. They were actually interested in what Rick and I, in our 300-square-foot factory, were making!

After we finished speaking, there was a roar of applause. Adam, the chef and kitchen director, placed his first order on the spot. Rick and I were ready to head straight to the inviting bar to celebrate, but before we could, Adam asked us to stay for dinner. How could we not? But how could we? We were broke, and although I just received a new American Express card in the mail, it was already maxed. Did we have to pay or were we guests? Reservations for dinner at Blue Hill at Stone Barns had to be made two months in advance, so we decided that it didn't matter; it would be worth the evening and worth the risk of a declined card. The hostess escorted us to a table in the corner closest to the kitchen. In the center of the room was a sixteen-foot table with a floral display that reached out from the center and up to the ceiling, bringing the surrounding outdoor colors into the dining room.

The caliber of the place, the commitment to sustainable farming, gardening, sourcing, and, of course, preparation and precision in cooking, were like nothing I'd ever seen. And they were inspired by what we were doing? Incredible. We were honored and knew we were in for a treat. "The chefs would like to prepare your meal. Anything you prefer not to have or are allergic to?" one of our five waiters asked. "Nope," we replied in unison. Thomas, the sommelier, arrived next. "We'd like to simply choose the wine for you two this evening to pair with each course." There were fourteen dishes to come, and I was ecstatic not to have to make any decisions. I was about to have the first best meal of my life. —*MM*

SPICED COCOA BUTTERNUT SQUASH SOUP

Serves 4

The sweetness of butternut squash lends itself nicely to a cacao nib–spice pairing.

Butternut squash	2 pounds
Yellow onion	1 medium
Garlic	2 cloves
Unsalted butter	1 tablespoon
Fresh ginger	2 tablespoons grated
Cocoa powder	2 teaspoons
Ground cinnamon	1 teaspoon
Serrano chile	½, chopped
Vegetable stock	4 cups
Sea salt	2 teaspoons
Cacao nibs	2 tablespoons
Olive oil	To garnish
Squash seeds	Toasted, to garnish

1. Peel and seed the butternut squash.
2. Chop squash into 1-inch cubes.
3. Roughly chop onion and garlic.
4. Sauté squash, onion, and garlic in butter over medium heat for 5 minutes.
5. Add ginger, cocoa powder, cinnamon, and serrano.
6. Sauté for another 5 minutes.
7. Add vegetable stock and bring to a simmer.
8. Let simmer until squash is fork-tender.
9. Purée mixture in a blender and season with salt.
10. Garnish with cacao nibs, olive oil, and toasted squash seeds.

CHOCOLATE BEET CAKE

Serves 12

Not only do the beets give the cake a rich, velvet-like color,
but they also provide depth of flavor.

/ /

Beets	5 medium
Unsalted butter	1 cup (2 sticks)
Dark chocolate	4 ounces, chopped
Brown sugar	1 cup
Eggs	3
All-purpose flour	2 cups
Baking soda	2 teaspoons
Sea salt	1 teaspoon

/ /

1. Preheat the oven to 350 degrees Fahrenheit.
2. Wash and rinse beets, wrap in foil, and roast in the oven for 45 minutes.
3. Peel the beets while warm and purée in blender. Set aside ½ cup purée for topping.
4. In double boiler melt 1 stick butter with the chocolate.
5. In bowl, cream the remaining stick butter with brown sugar until fluffy.
6. While whisking, add eggs one at a time to creamed butter mixture.
7. Add beet purée to melted chocolate mixture.
8. Combine both mixtures.
9. Add flour, baking soda, and salt.
10. Pour batter into 12-inch buttered loaf pan.
11. Bake for 45 minutes.
12. Top the cooled cake with the reserved beet purée.

RED WINE BONBONS

Makes 24

A full-bodied red wine works best here, as it won't be overpowered by the dark chocolate.
Try a Criollo-heavy chocolate with notes of dark fruit, like Madagascar.

///

GANACHE

Heavy cream	½ cup
Dark chocolate	6 ounces, chopped
Red wine	2 ounces (just over ⅓ cup)
Unsalted butter	1 tablespoon

COATING

Dark chocolate	8 ounces, melted and tempered (see page 9)

///

Make the Ganache

1. Bring cream to a boil in a saucepan.
2. Pour cream over chocolate in a heatproof bowl.
3. Let it sit and melt for 1 minute.
4. Stir with a spatula in tight circles from the center outward.
5. Slowly add red wine, stirring constantly to retain emulsification.
6. Let mixture cool to 108 degrees Fahrenheit. Test with an instant-read thermometer.
7. Add butter and stir until combined.
8. Shape ganache into marble-size spheres by rolling between your hands.

Coat the Bonbons

9. Using a dome-shaped confection mold, create shell of bonbons by pouring tempered chocolate into domes, covering them completely.
10. Turn mold upside down, pouring excess chocolate into a bowl, leaving an even coating on domes.
11. Refrigerate about 15 minutes to set.
12. Once set, add ganache, leaving room at top to coat.
13. Cool mold in refrigerator for 15 minutes.
14. Pour tempered chocolate over mold.
15. With spatula, spread evenly over mold, scraping away excess chocolate.
16. Let sit in fridge until bonbons pull away from mold, about 15 minutes.
17. Carefully tap mold on hard surface, allowing bonbons to release.

CHOCOLATE MOUSSE

Serves 6

Light and airy but also rich and luxurious.
Using world-class chocolate takes this dessert to new heights.

Water	¼ cup
Sugar	¼ cup
Dark chocolate	10 ounces, chopped
Egg yolks	4
Heavy cream	2 cups

---

1. Combine water and sugar in a saucepan and bring to a boil. Let cool.
2. Melt chocolate in a double boiler.
3. In a separate bowl on a double boiler, combine sugar syrup with egg yolks
and whisk until mixture thickens and becomes fluffy.
4. Mix in melted chocolate until smooth.
5. In a separate bowl, using a handheld mixer, whip heavy cream to soft peaks.
6. Mix one-third of the whipped cream into chocolate emulsion until combined.
7. Gently fold in remainder of whipped cream.

CHOCOLATE CRANBERRY PORK TENDERLOIN

Serves 6

The chocolate balances the tart cranberries with the savory pork.

///

CHOCOLATE CRANBERRY SAUCE

Pork chops	1½ pounds
Onion	1 medium
Garlic	1 clove
Unsalted butter	3 tablespoons
Red wine	3 cups
Chicken stock	4 cups
Cranberry juice	1 cup
Dried cranberries	½ cup
Sea salt	2 teaspoons
Black pepper	2 teaspoons
Sherry vinegar	1 tablespoon
Cacao nibs	½ cup

PORK TENDERLOIN

Pork tenderloin	1½ pounds
Sea salt	2 teaspoons
Black pepper	2 teaspoons
Unsalted butter	3 tablespoons

///

Make the Chocolate Cranberry Sauce
1. Cut pork chops into small bits.
2. Dice onion and garlic.
3. Sweat onion and garlic in butter over medium heat.
4. Add pork and sauté until pork is browned.
5. Deglaze pan with red wine and scrape the bits from bottom of pan.
6. Cook and reduce red wine by one-half.
7. Add stock and cranberry juice and stir.
8. Reduce liquid by one-half.
9. Strain the sauce and return to the saucepan. Bring to a simmer.
10. Add cranberries, salt, and pepper.
11. Add vinegar and cacao nibs.

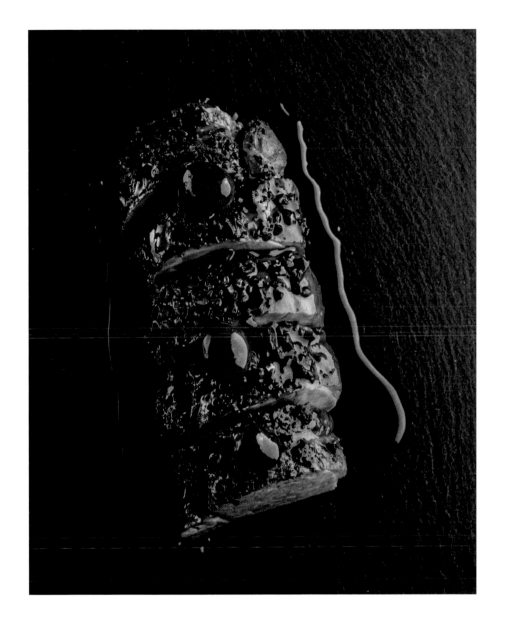

Make the Pork Tenderloin

12. Preheat oven to 325 degrees Fahrenheit.

13. Season pork with salt and pepper.

14. Melt and brown butter in a cast-iron pan over medium-high heat.

15. Place tenderloin in browned butter and sear all sides until golden brown.

16. Keeping tenderloin in the pan, place in oven for 10 minutes.

17. Glaze tenderloin by ladling sauce over top before slicing.

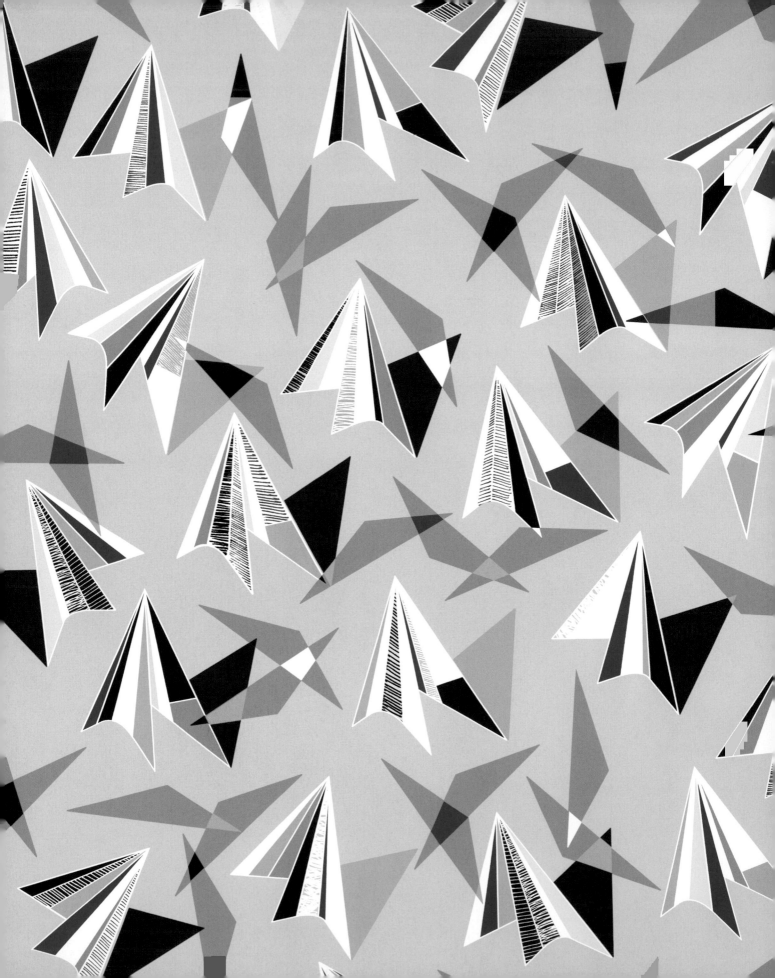

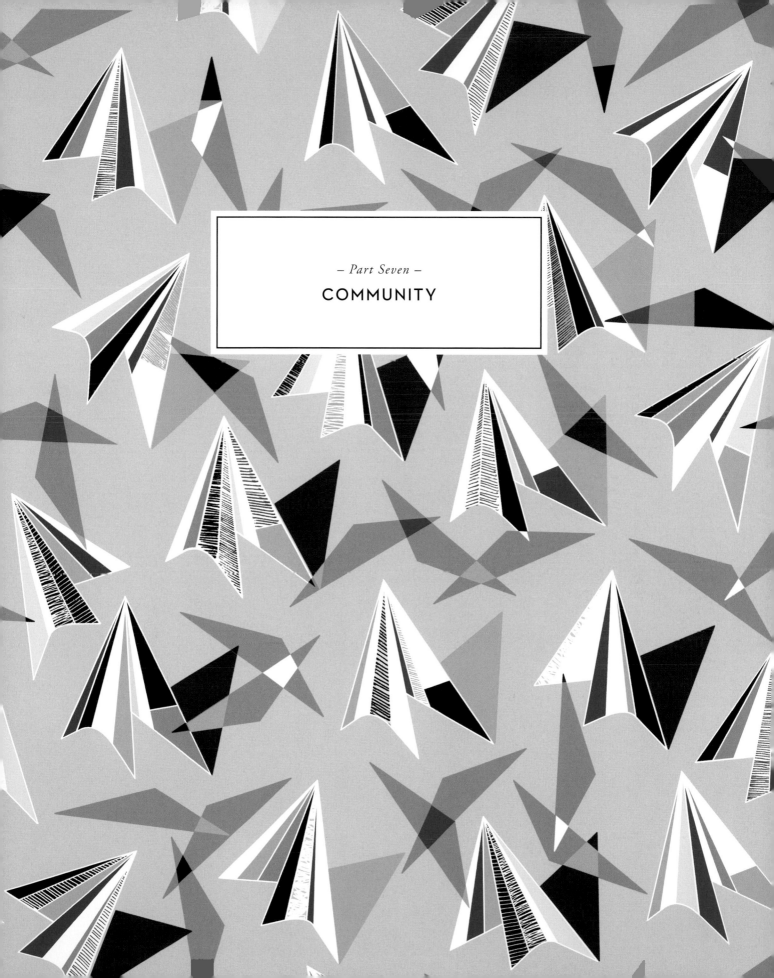

— Part Seven —

COMMUNITY

AN AMERICAN COLLABORATION

───────

*T*homas Jefferson and I came face to face in Monticello, Virginia, during a family road trip that began with a call from Alice Waters. We'd been to Nashville and drove back up through Virginia, where we found ourselves guests at Jefferson's famous estate. Home brewing, a collection of obscure wines, homegrown vegetables, an on-site smokehouse, and wall-to-wall taxidermy? Could it be that today's hip Brooklyn community is actually better described as Jeffersonian? A culture driven by curiosity, creativity, and utopian definitions of community, with all of the hypocrisies and contradictions that inevitably go along with such idealism?

Like Jefferson's America, Brooklyn is a borough filled with immigrants looking for a new world. More immigrants may be coming from the rural Midwest than from Italy, Poland, or Ireland these days, but the reasons are the same: opportunity. Many of the consequences are the same as well, among them cultural integration. My brother and I grew up in Iowa City in a family that would be considered a bit on the stoic side. A family that values a quiet, white-knuckled work ethic and a no-frills lifestyle. A practical family of handyman homeowners, well-kept Toyota Camrys, and manicured lawns. Toto, we're not in Kansas anymore.

I first became interested in Jefferson on a more spiritual level after reading *The Jefferson Bible,* a science-based version of the New Testament that he wrote during his presidency. Like many, I soon discovered and was drawn to his wide-ranging interests, particularly his interests in oenology, anthropology, and botany. I love the stories of Jefferson crawling around on hands and knees in the White House lobby, poring over dinosaur bones brought to him by Lewis and Clark on one of their many expeditions. This type of insatiable curiosity and sense of discovery inspire me.

On a quiet afternoon, I received a phone call from Alice Waters's assistant asking if I would call her at home immediately about a special chocolate bar she would like. Of course, I anxiously called her right away. We had met once or twice previously at food functions, but only very quickly and casually. Alice let me know that the chocolate she wanted would be given away at a beautiful dinner function that would take place on the grounds of Monticello and that all proceeds would go to the museum.

We were honored to be asked and overjoyed when we found out that the project was to be a collaboration with Maira Kalman, famed illustrator of many a *New Yorker* cover, who would design the custom wrapper. Maira's passion for Monticello and Jefferson is whimsical and infectious. Our conversations with Maira put Monticello on my must-do-immediately list. The picture she painted (quite literally) of Monticello was filled with colors, stories, and history, and I knew I would find great inspiration there.

It was a moody, rainy midsummer morning in the hills of Virginia. My wife and one-year-old son, Sebastian, and I had just driven most of the previous day from Nashville and had finally arrived. We parked and made a run to the nearest awning, to protect ourselves from what had now become a downpour. The visitor's center is a beautifully accommodating modern wooden structure filled with elegantly curated gifts, books, galleries, furniture, and wines. After purchasing our tickets, we boarded the shuttle bus to take us to the surprisingly modest, unfussy, Greek Revival brick home. This was not the home of a man who wanted to show

off his wealth; it was the home of someone who wanted to engage his guests in a conversation.

The home is set on a hillside, and the land surrounding it is expansive, manicured immediately around the structure but wild as far as the eye can see. In certain ways, Jefferson's home embodies the spirit of our chocolate factory. Jefferson's estate was in constant change. He continually evaluated improvements and potential changes to design, construction, and layout. His home was, in all regards, a living laboratory. Wings were added, rooms redesigned, and the grounds reconfigured. Beer was brewed, meats were smoked and cured, farming practices rethought. Jefferson himself designed not only the building but also the parquet floors, the parlor curtains, and various accessories, including a unique book holder that fits four books on a turntable, making each book accessible and open for reading wherever he left off.

Our team at Mast Brothers is forever eye-rolling at the daily change I live for. Some live in fear of it. I sprint into work with frenzied excitement over a change that must happen right now! "We are going to move the retail shop counters to the other side of the shop this morning!" Disrupting the daily routine is one of my favorite activities. Shake it up and evolve. Be fearless and experiment. Embrace continuous improvement in pursuit of ultimate simplicity. —RM

CHOCOLATE PECAN PIE

Serves 8

Deliciously gooey, with beautifully crunchy toasted pecans.

////////////////////////////////////

CRUST

Pecans	¼ cup
All-purpose flour	1 cup
Brown sugar	⅓ cup
Sea salt	½ teaspoon
Baking powder	¼ teaspoon
Unsalted butter	6 tablespoons (¾ stick), cut into cubes

FILLING

Unsalted butter	¼ cup (½ stick), melted
Brown sugar	½ cup
Sea salt	1 teaspoon
Eggs	2
Pecans	2 cups
Dark chocolate	5 ounces, chopped

////////////////////////////////////

Make the Crust

1. Preheat oven to 350 degrees Fahrenheit.

2. Place pecans on a baking sheet and toast for 10 minutes.

3. Mix flour, brown sugar, salt, baking powder, and toasted pecans in a food processor until coarse.

4. Add butter and combine.

5. Pat dough into a 9-inch round pie plate.

6. Bake for 15 minutes. Let cool.

Make the Filling

7. In a medium bowl, mix melted butter, brown sugar, and salt.

8. Add eggs, pecans, and chocolate and combine.

9. Pour mixture into crust.

10. Bake for 25 minutes. Let cool.

COCOA BALSAMIC VINAIGRETTE

Makes 1¼ cups

Splurge on a wonderful balsamic vinegar and local honey.
Serve with salads, fruits, and aged cheeses.

Fresh rosemary	½ sprig
Cacao nibs	1 tablespoon
Cocoa powder	2 teaspoons
Sea salt	2 teaspoons
Black pepper	1 teaspoon
Balsamic vinegar	¼ cup
Honey	2 teaspoons
Extra-virgin olive oil	1 cup

---

1. Remove rosemary leaves from stem and roughly chop.
2. Combine rosemary leaves, nibs, cocoa powder, salt, and pepper and grind in a mortar with a pestle.
3. Place ground ingredients in a medium bowl.
4. Add balsamic vinegar and honey and whisk.
5. Slowly add olive oil while whisking quickly to emulsify.
6. Store in a mason jar in the refrigerator for up to 1 week.

CHOCOLATE STOUT TRIFLE

Serves 10

A showstopper. Serve in individual glass bowls or one giant bowl and garnish with grated chocolate. Offer Chocolate Black Velvets (page 247) to round out the evening!

///

CAKE

Eggs	6
Sugar	2 cups
Cake flour	2 cups
Cocoa powder	¾ cup
Baking powder	2 teaspoons

MOUSSE

Dark chocolate	2½ ounces, chopped
Stout	1 cup
Sugar	¼ cup
Egg yolks	4
Heavy cream	1¾ cups

WHIPPED CREAM

Heavy cream	2 cups

///

Make the Cake

1. Preheat oven to 375 degrees Fahrenheit. Butter a 9-inch round cake pan.
2. In the bowl of a standing mixer, beat the eggs and sugar until fluffy.
3. Sift and mix in flour, cocoa powder, and baking powder.
4. Pour batter into the cake pan.
5. Bake for 30 minutes.

Make the Mousse

6. Melt chocolate in a double boiler.
7. In a separate pot, bring stout and sugar to a boil. Take off the heat and let cool.
8. Mix stout syrup with egg yolks in a clean double boiler, stirring constantly until mixture thickens.
9. In a large bowl, mix stout-egg mixture with melted chocolate until emulsified.
10. In the bowl of a standing mixer, whip heavy cream to soft peaks.
11. Mix one-third of whipped cream into mousse. Fold in remainder of whipped cream.

Make the Whipped Cream

12. In the bowl of a standing mixer, whip heavy cream to stiff peaks.

Assemble

13. Cut cake into thick slices and layer one-third of them in the bottom of a bowl.

14. Spread one-third of the mousse on top of the cake layer and cover that with one-third of the whipped cream.

15. Repeat twice to make three layers.

ALMOND CHOCOLATE CAKE

Serves 10

Use the recipe for ganache (see page 31) and top with crushed toasted almonds to finish.

Unsalted butter	1 cup (2 sticks)
Egg whites	8
Confectioners' sugar	2 cups
Almond flour	1½ cups
All-purpose flour	1 cup
Dark chocolate	8 ounces, chopped

1. Preheat oven to 325 degrees Fahrenheit.
2. In a saucepan, heat butter over medium heat until golden brown.
3. In a medium bowl, lightly whisk egg whites.
4. Add confectioners' sugar and both flours to egg whites and whisk to combine.
5. Melt chocolate in a double boiler.
6. Once cooled, add browned butter and melted chocolate to egg white mixture.
7. Whisk to combine thoroughly.
8. Pour the batter into a 9-inch round cake pan.
9. Bake for 25 minutes or until a toothpick inserted into the center comes out clean.

GERMAN CHOCOLATE CAKE

Serves 8

It turns out that German chocolate cake is not German at all. It was created by the American chocolate maker Sam German in 1852 and was originally referred to as "German's Chocolate Cake."

〜〜〜〜〜〜〜〜〜〜〜〜〜〜〜〜〜〜〜〜〜〜〜〜

CAKE

Water	½ cup
Dark chocolate	4 ounces, chopped
All-purpose flour	2 cups
Cocoa powder	¼ cup
Baking soda	1 teaspoon
Sea salt	1 teaspoon
Sugar	2 cups
Unsalted butter	1 cup (2 sticks), room temperature
Eggs	4, separated
Buttermilk	1 cup
Vanilla	1 teaspoon

FILLING

Sugar	2 cups
Evaporated milk	2 cups
Unsalted butter	1 cup (2 sticks)
Egg yolks	9
Coconut flakes	2½ cups
Pecans	2 cups, chopped
Dark chocolate	8 ounces, chopped

〜〜〜〜〜〜〜〜〜〜〜〜〜〜〜〜〜〜〜〜〜〜〜〜

Make the Cake

1. Preheat oven to 375 degrees Fahrenheit.
2. Bring water to boil and pour over chopped chocolate in bowl. Stir until smooth.
3. In separate bowl, combine flour, cocoa powder, baking soda, and salt.
4. In a standing mixer, beat sugar and butter until fluffy.
5. Add egg yolks, chocolate mixture, buttermilk, and vanilla.
6. Add flour mixture. Combine.
7. In separate bowl, beat egg whites to soft peaks.
8. Fold egg whites into batter.
9. Butter a 12-inch round cake pan, pour in batter, and bake for 50 minutes.

Make the Filling

10. In a saucepan, mix sugar, evaporated milk, butter, and egg yolks.

11. Stir and cook over low heat until mixture thickens. Take off heat.

12. Mix in coconut flakes, pecans, and chocolate.

Assemble

13. Cut the cake horizontally into 2 layers.

14. Spread filling between layers and on top of cake.

LUNCH BREAK

It started out of necessity. My brother and I were creating our company in our apartment on a shoestring budget, getting up early to discuss recipes, logos, missions, and farms. We needed a routine, a reward, and mainly a break.

Every last penny was going into our enterprise. We dug through our pockets: wrinkled receipts, paper clips, Post-it notes with illegible scribblings, and a couple of crumpled bills. It wasn't our first experience being essentially broke. We had become well-practiced masters of what we would call poor-man's pasta, one-hour stews, quarter casseroles, and anything we could throw together in a single pot. In constant conversation about our chocolate, Michael and I would walk to the supermarket with our meager savings to see how we could, once again, stretch each dollar to create something other than the same old lunch.

During this early, exciting, and stressful period, there was nothing quite like being able to take an hour in the middle of the day to relax, cook, sit down, and eat, enjoying each other's company and gaining the strength to discuss the day with a clear head and a full stomach.

The simple act of slowing down to cook and enjoy a decent lunch quickly became part of the fabric of our company's culture. For the first few years it was just my brother and me. It became routine, a ritual. A way for us to take stock in the importance of food, good ingredients, and sitting down together.

As our family at Mast Brothers has grown—with more staff, locations, products, sales, and departments—sitting down to lunch together in the midst of constant activity has become the one constant. During the daily production meeting, every morning, the final topic of discussion is: What's for lunch? Who is going to head to the supermarket? Now, on any given day, we have nearly twenty staff members gathered around a long table in a room dedicated to our daily ritual. Preparations often begin as early as 10 a.m., and the smell of lunch being prepared wafts through the entire building.

Chopped leeks and thick-cut strips of bacon with garlic render down with quartered Brussels sprouts. Basil we grow in the planters out front is washed, torn, and scattered throughout the layers of lasagna with ricotta cheese, heirloom tomatoes, and strips of prosciutto. Large bunches of kale are washed, massaged, stripped of their stems, and tossed with a vinaigrette made with balsamic vinegar, chocolate, olive oil, and orange. By this time, seventeen chocolate makers in white chef's jackets line up at the counter. Plates in hand, they watch the lasagna being transferred from the oven to a folded towel on the butcher-block counter.

As the lasagna cools briefly, heavy cream is poured over the Brussels sprouts, bringing the dish to a rich finish. The large cast-iron pan is brought alongside the lasagna, where it is stirred quickly with a large wooden spoon. The spoon is then offered to the first in line.

One by one, smiling, wide-eyed chocolate makers thank their colleagues for the incredible lunch as they fill their plates. The lunch table is long and white, with barn lights hanging from the ceiling highlighting the daily feast. Old wooden carnival chairs and beer on draft offer tired legs a rest. As the table fills, the conversation is good. Happy. Discussions of tasting notes, grinding times, and tempering are replaced by tales of last night's mishaps, dirty jokes, and new songs to download. In an era when lunch break often means a fast-food sandwich to go or a yogurt and soda at your desk, our lunch break is a refreshing disturbance in the middle of the day. It is rejuvenating, collegial, and delicious. *—RM*

RED DEVIL'S FOOD CAKE

Serves 10

Use freshly juiced beets for best results. Top with cream cheese filling (see page 71)
and garnish with cacao nibs and shaved chocolate.

//

CAKE

All-purpose flour	2½ cups
Sugar	1½ cups
Cocoa powder	2 tablespoons
Baking soda	1 teaspoon
Sea salt	1 teaspoon
Vegetable oil	1½ cups
Buttermilk	¾ cup
Beet juice	¼ cup
Eggs	3
White wine vinegar	1 teaspoon
Vanilla	1 teaspoon

//

1. Preheat oven to 350 degrees Fahrenheit.
2. In bowl, combine flour, sugar, cocoa powder, baking soda, and salt.
3. In separate bowl, whisk together vegetable oil, buttermilk, beet juice, eggs, vinegar, and vanilla.
4. Combine flour and oil mixtures and whisk until smooth.
5. Pour batter into a buttered 12-inch round cake pan.
6. Bake for 45 minutes.
7. Slice cooled cake horizontally into 2 layers.
8. Spread cream cheese filling (page 71) between layers.

CHOCOLATE BLACK VELVET

Serves 1

The original version of this dark-hued drink was invented in London in the late nineteenth century following the death of Prince Albert. We've amped it up with a touch of chocolate and a refreshing hint of orange.

Chocolate Syrup (page 17)	½ ounce
Stout	1 ounce
Champagne or sparkling wine	3 ounces
Orange bitters	1 dash
Orange zest	1 twist

1. Pour Chocolate Syrup into a Champagne glass.
2. Add stout.
3. Pour Champagne slowly over the back of a metal spoon into the glass.
4. Add bitters.
5. Garnish with orange zest.

SARAH BERNHARDT COOKIES

Makes 30

Made in honor of the celebrated actress, these are actually a
Danish invention and are often simply referred to as "Sarahs."

Egg whites	4
Granulated sugar	3 tablespoons
Confectioners' sugar	1½ cups
Almond flour	¾ cup
Dark chocolate	8 ounces, chopped, plus 1 pound, melted and tempered (see page 9)
Heavy cream	½ cup
Unsalted butter	2 tablespoons

1. Preheat oven to 300 degrees Fahrenheit.
2. In the bowl of a standing mixer, or in a medium bowl with a handheld mixer, beat egg whites to soft peaks, adding granulated sugar as you beat.
3. Slowly add ¾ cup confectioners' sugar and beat until glossy and firm.
4. In a separate bowl, combine flour and remaining confectioners' sugar.
5. Add almond-sugar mixture to egg mixture and stir until smooth and runny.
6. Pour into pastry bag and pipe coin-size circles onto a baking sheet.
7. Bake for 12 minutes.
8. Place 8 ounces chopped chocolate in a medium heatproof bowl.
9. In a saucepan, bring heavy cream to a boil.
10. Pour cream over chocolate.
11. Let it sit and melt for 1 minute.
12. Stir with a spatula in tight circles from the center outward.
13. Let mixture cool to 108 degrees Fahrenheit. Test with an instant-read thermometer.
14. Add butter and stir until combined.
15. Put ganache into a pastry bag and pipe on top of each cookie.
16. Place cookies on parchment-lined baking sheet in refrigerator until ganache sets.
17. Dip cookies in tempered chocolate. Let set.

CHOCOLATE SNOW CAPS

Makes 30

These cookies are as pretty to look at as they are delicious to eat.
Like peering over the snowcapped peaks of the Rocky Mountains from an airplane window.

Unsalted butter	¼ cup (½ stick), room temperature
Light brown sugar	⅔ cup
Eggs	2
All-purpose flour	½ cup
Cocoa powder	¼ cup
Baking powder	1 teaspoon
Sea salt	1 teaspoon
Dark chocolate	5 ounces, chopped
Whole milk	1 tablespoon
Confectioners' sugar	1 cup

1. Preheat oven to 350 degrees Fahrenheit.
2. In a medium bowl, cream butter and brown sugar.
3. Add eggs, flour, cocoa powder, baking powder, and salt and combine.
4. Add chocolate and milk and combine.
5. Cover with plastic wrap and refrigerate for 1 hour.
6. Roll into 1-inch balls and coat with confectioners' sugar.
7. Place 1½ inches apart on a baking sheet.
8. Bake for 12 minutes.

HOOTENANNIES

"I want to turn the clock back to when people lived in small villages and took care of each other."
—*Pete Seeger*

⁄⁄⁄⁄⁄⁄⁄⁄

*O*ur first real factory was located in Williamsburg, Brooklyn, on North 3rd Street between Wythe and Berry. It was nestled on the bottom floor of a turn-of-the-century spice factory, with a small brick-walled and wood-beamed storefront that we had outfitted with an old apothecary-style counter and shelving system. It was like a dream: Make the chocolate in the back, help customers in the front. A chocolate-making idyll from long ago was coming back!

To make ends meet, we worked long and hard hours. By eight o'clock at night we were hungry and tired but still had heaps of chocolate bars to wrap for the coming day. With sore backs and deep sighs, we would wonder how we could possibly make these evenings bearable. Inevitably, Michael and I would get on the horn, calling everyone we could think of. We would promise food, beer, and wine as payment for wrapping chocolate bars into the night and keeping us company. Friends always make things easier—not just the extra hands but also the jokes, the perspectives, and the company, not to mention the fact that we were quite proud of our new factory and wanted to show it off, to share it.

Michael would immediately begin cooking. Often our friends would bring various side dishes and we would provide the main course. I would run to the closest wine shop to see what deals I could strike on their best cheap wine, stopping by the bodega down the street to pick up as many beers as I could hold. A perpetual people-pleaser, I would reliably go over our budget for these get-togethers, caught up in the moment and the romanticism of impromptu late-night dinner parties filled with chocolate, laughter, and music.

Our friends Aaron and Carla would show up with good beer by the growler. We would set up our make-shift wrapping station near the entrance to our shop on a long, rustic teak table with reclaimed wood legs. The glass displays on the counter would be cleared, transforming the old apothecary furniture into a buffet table for serving dishes, wine bottles, glasses, and silverware.

The sound of the rain hitting the pavement and the large front windows was a soothing background to the ever-present folk music, bluegrass, and country being played on our iPod. Ralph Stanley, Pete Seeger, A. A. Bondy, Johnny Cash, and Waylon Jennings, along with local favorites the Dust Busters, Dough Rollers, and our good buddy Fletcher C. Johnson.

"You have gotta hear this," was the mantra, as we all fought for dibs on the next song, leaving a chocolate bar half wrapped as we darted to make the selection.

Ten o'clock passed, our quota of chocolate was wrapped for the following day, the bowls of roasted root vegetables, stews, and mashed potatoes were empty, but the beer and wine still flowed. As eleven o'clock approached our cozy little chocolate shop made another transformation, this time to a cozy little pub. More friends stopped by, bringing more friends and more wine. The conversations grew louder and so did the music. The urgency in which everyone *must hear this song now* grew to desperate levels. Political debates ensued, relationships began, ended, and were rekindled.

Many of the chocolate bars we had just wrapped were unwrapped and passed around.

Passersby peered in from under their umbrellas, seeing the crowd that had grown to more than twenty, eating, drinking, laughing, dancing, and singing. They were befuddled as to what exactly this place was. A café? A bar? Private club? "Nope, it's a chocolate shop!" someone excitedly said. "We open up tomorrow at noon."

As midnight approached, the wine ran dry and the thought of an early morning began to loom. Out on the sidewalk, everyone smoked their last cigarette, parted ways, and headed home.

What began as wrapping parties—a creative way for us to make and wrap enough chocolate to keep the doors open—slowly evolved to full-blown hootenannies, as we started calling them. Inspired by the lives of Pete Seeger, Woody Guthrie, Phil Ochs, Bob Dylan, and Carl Sandburg, we soon replaced the iPod with live music, playing host to dozens of musicians. We moved the long communal table from the nook to the center of the shop, and in the nook set up a stool, a microphone, and a couple of beat-up speakers. Friends and strangers alike would come to the factory after hours; donate a dish, potluck-style, to the long countertop; and enjoy incredible music, bottomless glasses of wine, and, of course, chocolate. Folk musicians, bluegrass players, country bands, singer-songwriters, jazz musicians, and classical musicians played in front of stacks of cacao covered in burlap. Butcher-block and stainless-steel tables were moved, making room for dancing and gathering. The crowds soon spilled onto the sidewalk. The London newspaper *The Guardian* declared Mast Brothers Chocolate shop the best place to hang out in New York City. A surprising declaration considering we were only open to the public on weekends!

Our chocolate shop was, is, and always will be a social gathering space. A space to celebrate food, music, community, and craft. I like to think that another Midwesterner turned New Yorker, Woody Guthrie, is smiling on us from the other side. —*RM*

BLACK FOREST CUPCAKES

Makes 12

Said to have been named after the mountainous Black Forest in southwestern Germany,
the cake (and these cupcakes) is traditionally topped with a maraschino cherry.

//

CUPCAKES

Unsalted butter	½ cup (1 stick)
Dark chocolate	2½ ounces, chopped
Granulated sugar	¾ cup
Cocoa powder	½ cup
Eggs	2
All-purpose flour	¾ cup
Baking powder	¾ teaspoon
Baking soda	½ teaspoon
Sea salt	½ teaspoon
Heavy cream	1 cup

FROSTING

Cream cheese	8 ounces
Confectioners' sugar	½ cup
Kirsch	¼ cup

GARNISH

Maraschino cherries	12

//

Make the Cupcakes

1. Preheat oven to 350 degrees Fahrenheit. Butter 12 muffin cups.
2. Melt butter and chocolate in a saucepan over low heat.
3. Add granulated sugar and cocoa powder.
4. Add eggs and combine.
5. Add flour, baking powder and soda, and salt.
6. Add cream and combine.
7. Pour the batter into the muffin cups.
8. Bake for 15 minutes.

Make the Frosting

9. In a medium bowl, using a handheld mixer, slowly whip the cream cheese until fluffy.

10. Add confectioners' sugar and kirsch and combine.

Assemble

11. Spread frosting on top of each cupcake.

12. Place 1 maraschino cherry on top of each cupcake.

MINNESOTA FUDGE CAKE

Serves 10

A heartwarming cake for a cold winter's night.

///////////////////////////////////////

CAKE

All-purpose flour	2½ cups
Granulated sugar	1¼ cups
Brown sugar	¾ cup
Cocoa powder	1 cup
Baking soda	2¼ teaspoons
Sea salt	1½ teaspoons
Buttermilk	2¼ cups
Unsalted butter	1 cup (2 sticks), room temperature
Eggs	2
Dark chocolate	6 ounces, chopped

FUDGE SAUCE

Dark chocolate	4 ounces, chopped
Unsalted butter	¼ cup (½ stick), room temperature
Confectioners' sugar	2 cups
Water	½ cup

///////////////////////////////////////

Make the Cake

1. Preheat oven to 350 degrees Fahrenheit.
2. Mix flour, both sugars, cocoa powder, baking soda, salt, buttermilk, butter, and eggs in a large bowl.
3. Whisk until incorporated.
4. Melt chocolate in a double boiler. Add to mixture.
5. Pour batter into Bundt pan.
6. Bake for 40 minutes.

Make the Fudge Sauce

7. Melt chocolate and butter in a double boiler.
8. Add confectioners' sugar and water and whisk until smooth.
9. Pour evenly over cooled cake.

CHOCOLATE CARAMEL TART

Serves 12

I used to make this tart in a beautiful Martha's Vineyard kitchen,
overlooking the Gay Head lighthouse and the majestic cliffs of Aquinnah.

///

CRUST

All-purpose flour	2 cups
Cocoa powder	½ cup
Sugar	3 tablespoons
Unsalted butter	1 cup (2 sticks), cubed
Egg yolks	2
Ice water	¼ cup

CARAMEL

Sugar	1½ cups
Heavy cream	½ cup
Sea salt	½ teaspoon, plus more to garnish
Unsalted butter	¼ cup (½ stick)
Crème fraîche	2 tablespoons

GANACHE

Heavy cream	½ cup
Dark chocolate	5 ounces, chopped

///

Make the Crust

1. Preheat oven to 350 degrees Fahrenheit.
2. In a food processor, pulse flour, cocoa powder, sugar, and butter until flaky.
3. Add egg yolks and ice water and mix just until dough forms.
4. Turn dough out onto work surface and knead by hand until smooth.
5. Let dough rest in refrigerator for 30 minutes.
6. Roll thinly to fit into a 12-inch tart pan.
7. If available, use pie weights set on a piece of parchment paper on top of the dough
to keep crust in place while baking.
8. Bake for 20 minutes. Let cool.

Make the Caramel

9. Cook sugar in a saucepan over medium-high heat until golden brown.

10. Add cream and bring to a simmer. Simmer for 5 minutes.

11. Add salt, butter, and crème fraîche.

12. Pour caramel onto crust, let cool, and allow to set.

Make the Ganache

13. Bring cream to a boil in a saucepan.

14. Pour over chocolate in a heatproof bowl.

15. Let it sit and melt for 2 minutes. Stir until emulsified.

16. Pour ganache over caramel and sprinkle with a touch of sea salt.

HOMEMADE S'MORES

Makes 12

We were inspired by these delicious confections that Blue Bottle Coffee creates with our chocolate. Here is our own take on this classic campfire treat.

///////////////////////////////////////

GRAHAM CRACKERS

Graham flour	2 cups
All-purpose flour	½ cup
Brown sugar	½ cup
Ground cinnamon	1 teaspoon
Baking powder	1 teaspoon
Baking soda	½ teaspoon
Sea salt	½ teaspoon
Unsalted butter	7 tablespoons, cut into small cubes
Molasses	3 tablespoons
Whole milk	2 tablespoons

FILLING

Marshmallows	At least 12
Dark chocolate	At least 12 (1-ounce) squares

///////////////////////////////////////

Make the Graham Crackers

1. Preheat oven to 350 degrees Fahrenheit.
2. Pulse both flours, sugar, cinnamon, baking powder and soda, and salt in a food processor.
3. Add butter. Pulse to combine.
4. Add molasses and milk and mix until smooth.
5. Remove dough from processor, wrap in plastic wrap, and refrigerate for 1 hour.
6. Roll dough to roughly ⅛-inch thickness and cut into 24 (2-inch) squares.
7. Using a fork, poke 10 holes into each cut square.
8. Bake for 12 minutes. Let cool.

Assemble

9. Preferably over open fire, lightly toast marshmallows.
10. While marshmallows are still hot, sandwich marshmallows and chocolate squares between crackers.

CRISPY TREATS

Serves 12

//

Unsalted butter	3 tablespoons
Marshmallows	10 ounces
Dark chocolate	5 ounces, roughly chopped
Rice Krispies	6 cups

//

1. Melt butter and marshmallows in a saucepan over medium heat.
2. Add chocolate and heat until slightly melted.
3. Place cereal in a bowl, pour in chocolate-marshmallow mixture, and combine.
4. Pour the mixture into a 2-inch-deep 9-inch square pan.
5. Let cool and cut into squares.

THANK YOU, VESA

⁄ ⁄ ⁄ ⁄ ⁄ ⁄ ⁄ ⁄

*M*aking chocolate, running a company, and writing this book are all collaborative efforts. We have had the good fortune to surround ourselves with brilliant people who have helped us lay our foundation and build. This book could not have been created without the exceptional talents, hard work, and leadership of our Executive Pastry Chef (and now, Director of Chocolate) Vesa Parviainen.

Vesa found us by way of Helsinki, Finland. After serving in the Finnish army and traveling the world with the Finnish professional basketball team for five seasons, he began a stunning culinary career. He began in 1998 washing dishes for the famed two-Michelin-star restaurant Chez Dominique, working his way up to Executive Pastry Chef in 2004. He held the position for three years until he left to open his own restaurant, Postres (Spanish for "desserts"), that same year. He served as its Executive Pastry Chef and led the restaurant to a Michelin star in 2008. Vesa left Postres in 2011 to come to Mast Brothers Chocolate, where he began as an apprentice.

Vesa, along with his team, has painstakingly assisted us with the writing, measuring, and testing of our recipes, while performing his regular duties at Mast Brothers. He is a true talent, a gentleman, a professional, and one of the hardest workers we have ever encountered. We thank him greatly.

THANK YOU, EVERYONE!

A very special thank-you, of course, needs to be given to our entire staff. Your hard work, support, and belief in our mission are a constant source of energy.

Thank you to Tuukka—your eye and innovation have made this book what it is. Thank you, Nita and Eino, for joining the adventure.

A very special thank-you to Michael Sand; without you there would be no book. Your mentorship, patience, and Ping-Pong ability are unmatched and greatly appreciated.

A huge thank-you from the bottom of our hearts to Katherine Cowles for her persistence and belief that ours was a story to be told. Thank you for championing our craft.

Thank you to our trusted partner and best friend, Jake Lodwick, for going with his gut and his taste buds.

Thank you to our wives, Natasha and Megan, for keeping us anchored in love. Thank you to Sebastian for making Daddy smile when he was working late.

A special thanks to Nathan Warkentin, Sean Walker, Conor Hagen, Derek Herbster, Thomas Keller, Mark London, and Linda Thompson.

You are all a part of our family and always will be. We couldn't have done this without you.

METRIC CONVERSIONS

WEIGHT FORMULAS

Ounces to grams—multiply ounces by 28.35
Pounds to grams—multiply pounds by 453.5
Pounds to kilos—multiply pounds by .45

Exact Equivalents

1 ounce	28.35 grams
1 pound	453.59 grams, .45 kilograms

Approximate Equivalents

¼ ounce	7 grams
½ ounce	14 grams
1 ounce	28 grams
1¼ ounces	35 grams
1½ ounces	40 grams
1⅔ ounces	45 grams
2 ounces	55 grams
2½ ounces	70 grams
4 ounces	112 grams
5 ounces	140 grams
8 ounces	228 grams
10 ounces	280 grams
15 ounces	425 grams
16 ounces (1 pound)	454 grams

TEMPERATURE FORMULA

Fahrenheit to centigrade—subtract 32
from Fahrenheit, multiply by 5, then
divide by 9. $(F-32) \times 5/9$

Approximate Equivalents

250°F	120°C
275°F	135°C
300°F	150°C
325°F	160°C
350°F	180°C
375°F	190°C
400°F	200°C
450°F	230°C

METRIC CONVERSIONS

VOLUME FORMULAS

Cups to milliliters—multiply cups by 2.4
Cups to liters—multiply cups by .24

Exact Equivalents

1 teaspoon	4.9 milliliters
1 tablespoon	14.8 milliliters
1 ounce	29.57 milliliters
1 cup	236.6 milliliters
1 pint	473.2 milliliters

Approximate Equivalents

1/4 cup	60 milliliters
1/3 cup	80 milliliters
1/2 cup	120 milliliters
2/3 cup	160 milliliters
3/4 cup	177 milliliters
1 cup	230 milliliters
1 1/4 cups	300 milliliters
1 1/2 cups	360 milliliters
1 2/3 cups	400 milliliters
2 cups	460 milliliters
2 1/2 cups	600 milliliters
3 cups	700 milliliters
4 cups (1 quart)	.95 liter
4 quarts (1 gallon)	3.8 liters

LENGTH FORMULA

Inches to centimeters—multiply inches by 2.54

INDEX

Page numbers in *italic* refer to photographs.

A

Agouti Cacao Farm (Belize), 45–46, *47*
almond(s):
    Chocolate Cake, *238*, 239
    Chocolate Granola, *164*, 165
    Classic Chocolate Brownies, *18*, 19
    Fruit & Nut Bark, *100*, 101
    Sarah Bernhardt Cookies, *248*, 249
    Toasted Almond Truffles, *128*, 129
arugula, in Cacao Nib Salad, *192*, 193

B

balsamic vinegar, in Cocoa Balsamic Vinaigrette, *234*, 235
Barbecue Sauce, Chocolate, *196*, 197
Barber, Dan and David, 216–17
Barragan, Daniel, 147
Bedford Cheese Shop (Brooklyn), 176, 177
beef:
    Cincinnati Chili, *198*, 199
    steaks, Cocoa Dry Rub for, *190*, 191
    Steak with Nibs & Peppercorns, *188*, 189
Beet Chocolate Cake, *220*, 221
beet juice, in Red Devil's Food Cake, *244*, 245
Belize, cacao farming in, 45–46, *47*
Black & White Cookies, 108–9, *109*
Black Forest Cupcakes, 254–55, *255*
Black Seal, 76, *77*, 91–93, *92*, 105–7, 135
Black Truffle Truffles, *214*, 215
Black Velvet, Chocolate, *246*, 247
Blueberry Chocolate Pie, 60, 61
Blue Hill at Stone Barns (Pocantico Hills, N.Y.), 216–17
Bonbons, Red Wine, *222*, 223
Boston Cream Pie, 82–83
Bourbon Chocolate Balls, *80*, 81
Bread, Chocolate, *114*, 115
Bread Pudding, Chocolate, *178*, 179
Brittle, Peanut Nib, *172*, 173

Brooklyn:
    community support for local businesses in, 176–77
    Jefferson's America compared to, 230
    locavore scene in, 75
    sailing cacao beans from Dominican Republic to, 75–76, 91–93, 105–7, 135
    waterfront of, 105–7
brownies:
    Chocolate, *18*, 19
    Marbled Cheesecake, *168*, 169
butchers, chocolate makers compared to, 187
butter, in Chocolate Butter Ganache Squares, *140*, 141
Buttercream, Chocolate, *124*, 125
Butternut Squash Soup, Spiced Cocoa, *218*, 219

C

cacao:
    disposing of shells, 136, 176
    farming in Belize, 45–46, *47*
    making craft chocolate with, 135–36
    roasting, 135–36
    sailing from Dominican Republic to Brooklyn, 75–76, 91–93, 105–7, 135
    varietals of, 121
    winnowing machine for, 136
cacao nib(s):
    Cocoa Dry Rub, *190*, 191
    Country Pâté, *194*, 195
    making craft chocolate with, 136
    Orange Nib–Crusted Salmon, 212–13, *213*
    Peanut Brittle, *172*, 173
    Pork Sausage, *200*, 201
    Salad, *192*, 193
    Scallops, *88*, 89
    Steak with Peppercorns &, *188*, 189
cakes:
    Almond Chocolate, *238*, 239
    Black Forest Cupcakes, 254–55, *255*
    Boston Cream Pie, 82–83

cakes (*cont.*)
    chocolate, in Chocolate Stout Trifle, 236–37, *237*
    Chocolate Beet, *220*, 221
    Chocolate Cupcakes, *30*, 31
    Chocolate Date, *174*, 175
    Chocolate Lava, *132*, 133
    Chocolate Layer, *126*, 127
    Chocolate Marble, 78–79, *79*
    Chocolate Roll, *166*, 167
    Chocolate Rum, *96*, 97
    Chocolate Strawberry Shortcake, *180*, 181
    Dark & Stormy Chocolate, *94*, 95
    Flourless Chocolate, *152*, 153
    German Chocolate, 240–41, *241*
    Minnesota Fudge, *256*, 257
    Red Devil's Food, *244*, 245
    Sour Cream Fudge, *182*, 183
    Whoopie Pies, *70*, 71
    Yellow, with Chocolate Frosting, *110*, 111
candies and confections:
    Black Truffle Truffles, *214*, 215
    Chocolate Bourbon Balls, *80*, 81
    Chocolate Butter Ganache Squares, *140*, 141
    Chocolate Caramels with Sea Salt, *98*, 99
    Chocolate-Covered Pretzels, 84–85, *85*
    Chocolate Crunch, *112*, 113
    Chocolate Fudge, *64*, 65
    Chocolate Turtles, *62*, 63
    Classic Chocolate Truffles, *138*, 139
    Fruit & Nut Bark, *100*, 101
    Peanut Butter Cups, *24*, 25
    Peanut Nib Brittle, *172*, 173
    Red Wine Bonbons, *222*, 223
    Stumptown Mocha Truffles, *116*, 117
    Toasted Almond Truffles, *128*, 129
caramel(s):
    Chocolate Caramels with Sea Salt, *98*, 99
    Chocolate Caramel Tart, 258–59, *259*
    Hot Caramel Fudge Sauce, *156*, 157
Carrol, Joe, 176–77
Champagne, in Chocolate Black Velvet, *246*, 247
Cheesecake Brownies, Marbled, *168*, 169
chicken:
    Cocoa Coq au Vin, 208–9, *209*
    Savory Chocolate Cream Sauce for, *144*, 145
Chili, Cincinnati, *198*, 199
chocolate:
    butchers compared to makers of, 187
    craft, 7, 28, 135–36
    dark, choosing, 7
    public's lack of knowledge about making of, 27, 28

    tempering, 9
    wrapping, 146–47, 252–53
    see also cacao
Chocolate, Maple & Pecan Cookies, *154*, 155
Chocolate Barbecue Sauce, *196*, 197
Chocolate Beet Cake, *220*, 221
Chocolate Black Velvet, *246*, 247
Chocolate Blueberry Pie, *60*, 61
Chocolate Bourbon Balls, *80*, 81
Chocolate Bread, *114*, 115
Chocolate Bread Pudding, *178*, 179
Chocolate Buttercream, *124*, 125
Chocolate Butter Ganache Squares, *140*, 141
Chocolate Caramels with Sea Salt, *98*, 99
Chocolate Caramel Tart, 258–59, *259*
chocolate chip:
    Cookies, *20*, 21
    Double Chocolate Chip Cookies, *40*, 41
    & Ricotta Pancakes, *102*, 103
Chocolate-Covered Pretzels, 84–85, *85*
Chocolate Cranberry Pork Tenderloin, 226–27, *227*
Chocolate Cream Pie, 142–43, *143*
Chocolate Crunch, *112*, 113
Chocolate Cupcakes, *30*, 31
Chocolate Date Cake, *174*, 175
Chocolate Egg Cream, 151
Chocolate Frosting, *110*, 111, *126*, 127
Chocolate Fudge, *64*, 65
Chocolate Gingersnaps, *86*, 87
Chocolate Glaze, 82, 83
Chocolate Granola, *164*, 165
Chocolate Hazelnut Spread, *148*, 149
Chocolate Ice Cream, *22*, 23
Chocolate Icing, 108, 109, *109*
Chocolate Lava Cake, *132*, 133
Chocolate Layer Cake, *126*, 127
Chocolate Marble Cake, 78–79, *79*
Chocolate Meringue Pie, 184–85, *185*
Chocolate Milk, *16*, 17
Chocolate Milk Shakes, *32*, 33
Chocolate Mousse, *224*, 225
Chocolate Oatmeal Cookies, *130*, 131
Chocolate Peanut Butter Cookies, *68*, 69
Chocolate Pecan Pie, *232*, 233
Chocolate Pots de Crème, *210*, 211
Chocolate Pudding, *38*, 39
Chocolate Roll, *166*, 167
Chocolate Rum Cake, *96*, 97
Chocolate Sauce, *66*, 67
Chocolate Snow Caps, *250*, 251

Chocolate Soda, *34*, 35
Chocolate Soufflé, *206*, 207
Chocolate Stout Trifle, 236–37, *237*
Chocolate Strawberry Shortcake, *180*, 181
Chocolate Syrup, 17, 33, 35, 151
Chocolate Turtles, *62*, 63
Cincinnati Chili, *198*, 199
Classic Chocolate Brownies, *18*, 19
Classic Chocolate Truffles, *138*, 139
Classic Hot Cocoa, *54*, 55
cocoa:
    Balsamic Vinaigrette, *234*, 235
    Classic Hot Cocoa, *54*, 55
    Coq au Vin, 208–9, *209*
    Dry Rub, *190*, 191
    Spiced Cocoa Butternut Squash Soup, *218*, 219
coconut flakes, in German Chocolate Cake, 240–41, *241*
coffee beans, in Stumptown Mocha Truffles, *116*, 117
confections, *see* candies and confections
Cook, Stephen and Sharon, 57, 58
cookies:
    Black & White, 108–9, *109*
    Chocolate, Maple & Pecan, *154*, 155
    Chocolate Chip, *20*, 21
    Chocolate Gingersnaps, *86*, 87
    Chocolate Oatmeal, *130*, 131
    Chocolate Peanut Butter, *68*, 69
    Chocolate Snow Caps, *250*, 251
    Double Chocolate Chip, *40*, 41
    Sarah Bernhardt, *248*, 249
Coq au Vin, Cocoa, 208–9, *209*
Country Pâté, Cacao, *194*, 195
craft chocolate, 7
    authors' resolve to make, 28
    making, 135–36
cranberries, dried:
    Chocolate Cranberry Pork Tenderloin, 226–27, *227*
    Chocolate Granola, *164*, 165
    Fruit & Nut Bark, *100*, 101
cream cheese:
    Filling, *70*, 71, 167
    Kirsch Frosting, 254, 255, *255*
Cream Pie, Chocolate, 142–43, *143*
Cream Sauce, Savory Chocolate, *144*, 145
Criollo cocoa beans, 121
Crispy Treats, *262*, 263
crusts:
    Chocolate, 61, 142, 184, 258

Pecan, 233
Tart, 171
cupcakes:
    Black Forest, 254–55, *255*
    Chocolate, *30*, 31

D
Dark & Stormy Chocolate Cake, *94*, 95
dark chocolate, choosing, 7
Date Chocolate Cake, *174*, 175
Dominican Republic, sailing cacao to Brooklyn from, 75–76, 91–93, 105–7, 135
Double Chocolate Chip Cookies, *40*, 41
Drinking Chocolate, *50*, 51
drinks:
    Chocolate Black Velvet, *246*, 247
    Chocolate Egg Cream, 151
    Chocolate Milk, *16*, 17
    Chocolate Milk Shakes, *32*, 33
    Chocolate Soda, *34*, 35
    Classic Hot Cocoa, *54*, 55
    Drinking Chocolate, *50*, 51
    Mayan Hot Chocolate, *48*, 49

E
Egg Cream, Chocolate, 151

F
fat content of chocolate, 7
fish and seafood:
    Cacao Nib Scallops, *88*, 89
    Orange Nib–Crusted Salmon, 212–13, *213*
Flourless Chocolate Cake, *152*, 153
Forastero cocoa beans, 121
French Laundry (Yountville, Calif.), 205
frisée, in Cacao Nib Salad, *192*, 193
frostings:
    Chocolate, *110*, 111, *126*, 127
    Chocolate Buttercream, *124*, 125
    Cream Cheese & Kirsch, 254, 255, *255*
    Ganache, *30*, 31
    Sour Cream, *182*, 183
Frozen Chocolate Pops, *36*, 37
Fruit & Nut Bark, *100*, 101
fudge:
    Chocolate, *64*, 65
    Hot Caramel Fudge Sauce, *156*, 157
    Minnesota Fudge Cake, *256*, 257
    Sauce, *256*, 257
    Sour Cream Fudge Cake, *182*, 183

G
Ganache, *30*, 31
  Black Truffle Truffles, *214*, 215
  Chocolate Butter Ganache Squares, *140*, 141
  Chocolate Caramel Tart, 258–59, *259*
  Chocolate Meringue Pie, 184–85, *185*
  Raspberry Rose Chocolate Tart, *170*, 171
  Red Wine Bonbons, *222*, 223
  Stumptown Mocha Truffles, *116*, 117
  Toasted Almond Truffles, *128*, 129
German Chocolate Cake, 240–41, *241*
ginger, in Dark & Stormy Chocolate Cake, *94*, 95
Gingersnaps, Chocolate, *86*, 87
glazes:
  Chocolate, *82*, 83
  Rum, *96*, 97
Goldberg, Arthur J., 75–76
Graham Crackers, 261
  Homemade S'Mores, *260*, 261
growing one's own food, 13–15

H
Hagen, Conor, 76
hazelnut(s):
  Chocolate Bread, *114*, 115
  Chocolate Hazelnut Spread, *148*, 149
  Classic Chocolate Brownies, *18*, 19
  Fruit & Nut Bark, *100*, 101
Homemade S'Mores, *260*, 261
hootenannies, at Mast Brothers factory, 252–53
Hot Caramel Fudge Sauce, *156*, 157
hot chocolate:
  Drinking Chocolate, *50*, 51
  Mayan, *48*, 49
Hot Cocoa, Classic, *54*, 55

I
ice cream:
  Chocolate, *22*, 23
  Chocolate Milk Shakes, *32*, 33
  Hot Caramel Fudge Sauce for, *156*, 157
Icings, Chocolate & White, 108, 109, *109*

J
Jefferson, Thomas, 230–31

K
Kalman, Maira, 230
Keller, Thomas, 1–2, 205
Kennedy, John F., 57
Kirsch & Cream Cheese Frosting, 254, 255, *255*

L
Lava Cake, Chocolate, *132*, 133
Lee, Cory, 205
Loftfield, Captain Eric, *74*, 75, 76, 91–93
Loftfield, Curtis, 93
lunch breaks, at Mast Brothers Chocolate, 243

M
Maine coast, vacationing on, 57–58
Maine Sea Salt Company, 57, 58
maple sugar, in Chocolate, Maple & Pecan Cookies,
  154, 155
Marble Cake, Chocolate, 78–79, *79*
Marbled Cheesecake Brownies, *168*, 169
Marlow & Sons, 176, 177
marshmallows:
  Crispy Treats, *262*, 263
  Homemade S'Mores, *260*, 261
Mast Brothers Chocolate:
  community support for, 176–77
  first factories of, 121–23, 252
  genesis of, 27–28, 75–76, 121–23, 161–62, 176–77
  hootenannies at, 252–53
  Jefferson's home compared to, 230–31
  Keller's visit to, 205
  lunch breaks at, 243
  making craft chocolate at, 135–36
  sailing cacao beans from Dominican Republic for,
    75–76, 91–93, 105–7, 135
  selling to public begun by, 161–62, 176–77
  traditional butcher shop as model for, 187
  wrappers and labels for, 146–47
Mayan Hot Chocolate, *48*, 49
meat:
  Cacao Country Pâté, *194*, 195
  Cacao Nib Sausage, *200*, 201
  Chocolate Barbecue Sauce for, *196*, 197
  Chocolate Cranberry Pork Tenderloin, 226–27, *227*
  Cincinnati Chili, *198*, 199
  Cocoa Dry Rub for, *190*, 191
  Savory Chocolate Cream Sauce for, *144*, 145
  Steak with Nibs & Peppercorns, *188*, 189
Meringue Pie, Chocolate, 184–85, *185*
Mexican:
  Mayan Hot Chocolate, *48*, 49
  Mole Sauce, 52–53, *53*
milk:
  Chocolate, *16*, 17
  Chocolate Egg Cream, 151
  Chocolate Milk Shakes, *32*, 33
  Drinking Chocolate, *50*, 51

Minnesota Fudge Cake, *256*, 257
Mocha Truffles, Stumptown, *116*, 117
Mole Sauce, 52–53, *53*
Monticello, Va., 230–31
mousse:
    Chocolate, *224*, 225
    Chocolate Stout Trifle, 236–37, *237*

O
oats, rolled:
    Chocolate Granola, *164*, 165
    Chocolate Oatmeal Cookies, *130*, 131
orange(s):
    Cacao Nib Salad, *192*, 193
    Chocolate Black Velvet, *246*, 247
    Nib–Crusted Salmon, 212–13, *213*

P
Pancakes, Chocolate Chip & Ricotta, *102*, 103
Park Slope Food Coop (Brooklyn), 176, 177
Parviainen, Vesa, *264*, 265
pasta, Savory Chocolate Cream Sauce for, *144*, 145
Pastry Cream, 82, 83
Pâté, Cacao Country, *194*, 195
peanut butter:
    Chocolate Cookies, *68*, 69
    Chocolate Crunch, *112*, 113
    Cups, *24*, 25
Peanut Nib Brittle, *172*, 173
pecan(s):
    Chocolate Bourbon Balls, *80*, 81
    Chocolate Granola, *164*, 165
    Chocolate & Maple Cookies, *154*, 155
    Chocolate Pecan Pie, *232*, 233
    Chocolate Turtles, *62*, 63
    Classic Chocolate Brownies, *18*, 19
    Fruit & Nut Bark, *100*, 101
    German Chocolate Cake, 240–41, *241*
Peppercorns, Steak with Nibs &, *188*, 189
Per Se (New York), 205
pies:
    Chocolate Blueberry, *60*, 61
    Chocolate Cream, 142–43, *143*
    Chocolate Meringue, 184–85, *185*
    Chocolate Pecan, *232*, 233
pistachios, in Fruit & Nut Bark, *100*, 101
Pop, Eladio, 45–46, *47*
Pops, Frozen Chocolate, *36*, 37
pork:
    Cacao Country Pâté, *194*, 195
    Cacao Nib Pork Sausage, *200*, 201

Chocolate Cranberry Pork Tenderloin,
    226–27, *227*
    Savory Chocolate Cream Sauce for, *144*, 145
Pots de Crème, Chocolate, *210*, 211
Pretzels, Chocolate-Covered, 84–85, *85*
puddings:
    Chocolate, *38*, 39
    Chocolate Bread, *178*, 179
puffed rice cereal:
    Chocolate Crunch, *112*, 113
    Rice Krispies, in Crispy Treats, *262*, 263

R
raisins:
    Chocolate Bread, *114*, 115
    Chocolate Rum Cake, *96*, 97
Raspberry Rose Chocolate Tart, *170*, 171
Red Devil's Food Cake, *244*, 245
Red Wine Bonbons, *222*, 223
ribs, Cocoa Dry Rub for, *190*, 191
Rice Krispies, in Crispy Treats, *262*, 263
Ricotta & Chocolate Chip Pancakes, *102*, 103
Roll, Chocolate, *166*, 167
rose water, in Raspberry Rose Chocolate Tart, *170*,
    171
rubs:
    Cocoa Dry, *190*, 191
    Orange Nib, 212, 213
rum:
    Chocolate Rum Cake, *96*, 97
    Dark & Stormy Chocolate Cake, *94*, 95
    Glaze, *96*, 97

S
salads:
    Cacao Nib, *192*, 193
    Cocoa Balsamic Vinaigrette for, *234*, 235
Salmon, Orange Nib–Crusted, 212–13, *213*
salt:
    Chocolate Caramels with Sea Salt, *98*, 99
    from Maine Sea Salt Company, 57, 58
Sarah Bernhardt Cookies, *248*, 249
sauces:
    Chocolate, *66*, 67
    Chocolate Barbecue, *196*, 197
    Chocolate Cranberry, 226
    Fudge, *256*, 257
    Hot Caramel Fudge, *156*, 157
    Mole, 52–53, *53*
    Savory Chocolate Cream, *144*, 145
Sausage, Cacao Nib Pork, *200*, 201

savories:
    Cacao Country Pâté, *194*, 195
    Cacao Nib Pork Sausage, *200*, 201
    Cacao Nib Salad, *192*, 193
    Cacao Nib Scallops, *88*, 89
    Chocolate Barbecue Sauce, *196*, 197
    Chocolate Cranberry Pork Tenderloin, 226–27, *227*
    Chocolate Cream Sauce, *144*, 145
    Cincinnati Chili, *198*, 199
    Cocoa Balsamic Vinaigrette, *234*, 235
    Cocoa Coq au Vin, 208–9, *209*
    Cocoa Dry Rub, *190*, 191
    Orange Nib–Crusted Salmon, 212–13, *213*
    Spiced Cocoa Butternut Squash Soup, *218*, 219
    Steak with Nibs & Peppercorns, *188*, 189
Scallops, Cacao Nib, *88*, 89
seafood, *see* fish and seafood
Seeger, Pete, 252, 253
seltzer:
    Chocolate Egg Cream, 151
    Chocolate Soda, *34*, 35
seven crowns, 1, 5
Shaw, George Bernard, 13
Shortcake, Chocolate Strawberry, *180*, 181
S'Mores, Homemade, *260*, 261
snacks:
    Chocolate Crunch, *112*, 113
    Chocolate Granola, *164*, 165
Soda, Chocolate, *34*, 35
Soufflé, Chocolate, *206*, 207
Soup, Spiced Cocoa Butternut Squash, *218*, 219
Sour Cream Fudge Cake, *182*, 183
Spiced Cocoa Butternut Squash Soup, *218*, 219
spices:
    Chocolate Gingersnaps, *86*, 87
    Cocoa Dry Rub, *190*, 191
    Dark & Stormy Chocolate Cake, *94*, 95
    Orange Nib Rub, 212, 213
spinach, baby, in Cacao Nib Salad, *192*, 193
Sponge Cake, in Boston Cream Pie, 82–83
Spread, Chocolate Hazelnut, *148*, 149
Spuyten Duyvil (microbrewery), 176–77
steak:
    Cocoa Dry Rub for, *190*, 191
    with Nibs & Peppercorns, *188*, 189
Stinky Brooklyn, 176, 177
stout:
    Chocolate Black Velvet, *246*, 247
    Chocolate Trifle, 236–37, *237*

Strawberry Chocolate Shortcake, *180*, 181
Stumptown Mocha Truffles, *116*, 117
sugar, organic cane, making craft chocolate with, 136
Syrup, Chocolate, 17, 33, 35, 151

T
Tarlow, Andrew, 177
tarts:
    Chocolate Caramel, 258–59, *259*
    Raspberry Rose Chocolate, *170*, 171
tempering chocolate, 9
Toasted Almond Truffles, *128*, 129
Trifle, Chocolate Stout, 236–37, *237*
Trinitario cocoa beans, 121
truffle oil, in Black Truffle Truffles, *214*, 215
truffles (confections):
    Black Truffle, *214*, 215
    Chocolate, Classic, *138*, 139
    Mocha, Stumptown, *116*, 117
    Toasted Almond, *128*, 129
Turtles, Chocolate, *62*, 63

V
vanilla wafer cookies, in Chocolate Bourbon Balls, *80*, 81
veal, Savory Chocolate Cream Sauce for, *144*, 145
Vinaigrette, Cocoa Balsamic, *234*, 235
Vitray, George, 176

W
Waters, Alice, 230
White Icing, 108, 109, *109*
wholesale accounts, 176
Whoopie Pies, *70*, 71
wine:
    Red Wine Bonbons, *222*, 223
    sparkling, in Chocolate Black Velvet, *246*, 247
winnowing machine, 136
wrapping chocolate, 146–47
    hootenannies and, 252–53

Y
yellow cake:
    with Chocolate Frosting, *110*, 111
    Chocolate Marble Cake, 78–79, *79*
Yoder, Lu, 76